How to Build Communication Success in Your School

This book provides a step-by-step guide to achieve best practice communication within schools. Communication is a critical component in building strong partnerships with parents, attracting and retaining the best teachers, building and protecting a school's reputation and, ultimately, in ensuring that students can be at their best.

Aligned to the National Standards of Excellence for Headteachers (2015), as well as Ofsted and the Independent Schools Inspectorate requirements, it provides an 'inside out' approach to create and communicate a compelling vision, building leadership communication skills and supporting the day-to-day management of communication in schools.

Full of practical strategies, audit tools and planning materials to help develop your communication approach, this guide covers key topics such as:

- attracting and retaining the best teachers;

- improving the effectiveness of leadership and management;

- building the reputation of the school;

- working with parents; and

- knowing what to do in a crisis.

How to Build Communication Success in Your School is essential reading for headteachers, school leaders and all those interested in education management and leadership.

Karen Dempster is a director of Fit2Communicate, UK. She also has a background in corporate and not-for-profit communication.

Justin Robbins is a director of Fit2Communicate, UK. He specialises in internal and change-focused communication.

How to Build Communication Success in Your School

A Guide for School Leaders

Karen Dempster and Justin Robbins

Routledge
Taylor & Francis Group

LONDON AND NEW YORK

First published 2017
by Routledge
2 Park Square, Milton Park, Abingdon, Oxon OX14 4RN

and by Routledge
711 Third Avenue, New York, NY 10017

Routledge is an imprint of the Taylor & Francis Group, an informa business

© 2017 Karen Dempster and Justin Robbins

British Library Cataloguing in Publication Data
A catalogue record for this book is available from the British Library

Library of Congress Cataloging in Publication Data
A catalog record for this book has been requested

ISBN: 978-1-138-24086-5 (hbk)
ISBN: 978-1-138-24087-2 (pbk)
ISBN: 978-1-315-28217-6 (ebk)

Typeset in Melior
by Saxon Graphics Ltd, Derby

Dedication
We dedicate this book to all teachers who are passionate about improving the lives of students and making our world a better place for the future.

Contents

Preface

Let's face it: everyone complains about communication. And that includes communication in organisations, including schools. Over the past 20 or so years, there has been a focus on improving communication in the business world, with great results. But what does good school communication actually look like? And why does it matter? What difference would good communication ultimately make to the success of a school and its students? Many schools that we have spoken to are doing what we would call 'hygiene communications'. These are the communications they have to do for the school to function. Messages to parents about sports day, parent evenings and staff notices are examples. Some schools do hygiene communications better than others. At their best they ensure parents don't miss important deadlines and students are where they need to be at the right time in the right uniform! Even hygiene communications are often done badly, resulting in frustration and a lack of interest in messages coming out of a school.

These aren't the type of communications that make a big difference though. They don't help anyone to understand a school's vision and know how it stands out from the crowd. They don't encourage teachers to stay with a school rather than walk away in pursuit of other careers. They don't fully engage parents to partner with schools to achieve the student outcomes we all hope for. In fact, how to communicate well is not even a part of a teacher's training path.

But we all know that communication is absolutely critical. It's proven, and yet, more often than not, it is the missing ingredient for many schools. Schools that take a structured and planned approach to communication within the school, with parents and the broader community, will have more engaged teachers, better involved parents and less of a need to market themselves. Who wouldn't want this for their school?

Parents are constantly bombarded with information from multiple sources in their lives. In a busy day how can a school ensure parents read what is important and often critical for their own child, when they are receiving several emails from school every day?

Schools are constantly playing catch up with technology. New ways of communicating are emerging nearly every day. Schools don't have the time or resources available to even try to understand how technology can fully support their communication. Often technology is implemented without an understanding of what return this will deliver on their investment. With funding being increasingly stretched this is not a good outcome.

So where do we come into all of this? Importantly, we are two parents who want the best for our school-age children. We are on the receiving end of school communications, and hear what other parents think on a daily basis. We have combined this practical experience with many years' of working in the corporate world – in marketing, public relations and internal communications. We have a shared passion for improving education through great communication. We started to see how our experience could make a huge difference when it came to school communication.

We have gathered input from teachers, headteachers and parents, to ensure that what we share in this book is based on reality, to develop a step-by-step approach to achieving better academic results (and happier teachers and students) through effective communication. We're now also working directly with schools.

We increasingly recognised the need for a new way to market schools (when competition is increasing), to engage teachers (when too many are leaving the profession) and to support schools in taking some of the pressure off during a period of major change for education.

This book is intended to address a clear gap and opportunity for schools. It explains in very practical terms exactly what good school communication looks like for teachers and parents. It will take you through the process of thinking about how your school communicates. It explains the process of planning what to say and when. It starts by helping you to understand how you are currently communicating so you have a realistic starting point, through to taking action by delivering your communication plan and keeping this going for the long term.

We hope this book makes a real difference; that's why we wrote it. We want to work with schools, headteachers and teachers to improve student outcomes, through this book, through online materials and through working hand-in-hand with individual schools. And at the end of the day, we have a vested interest in its success; we want our children to benefit from better communication in schools.

Thank you to everyone who made it possible: our friends, family and the wonderful teachers that we have encountered.

Foreword

"As an experienced teacher and qualified headteacher, I know the value of good communication. Sadly, there is little support for those in education to develop their communication skills, in the way that people in industry do. This book will give educationalists a step up and move our schools forward to achieve better student outcomes."

Joe Blaney
Apple Distinguished Educator, BA QTS, NPQH

"As a headteacher for 6 years, I've always believed in the value of great communication. But we all know that the pressures of the day job can push this down the priority list. We need to invest time in building support for our school visions and creating advocates among all of our school audiences. I'll definitely be putting the advice in this book into action."

Lisa Croke
B.Ed (Hons), MA Education, NPQH

Introduction

As a school leader or an aspiring headteacher, you already know that communication is important, because you are reading this book. That's a great start. You may be struggling to know where to start in improving communication with parents or even to deal with their 'feedback'. Or maybe you would like to develop your personal communication skills or to motivate and inspire other teachers. This book will put you on the right path in all of these areas and more.

It will help you to understand just how powerful communication can be for any school, whether your school is state sector or fee paying. It explains in simple everyday language, how to find the balance between too much and not enough communication for your school. It will enable you to communicate with meaning in ways that connect you with your audiences. It will help you to get the message right with your staff, parents and other key school audiences such as the Board of Governors and the local media.

And what will be the end result of putting this into practice? You'll have a teaching team that is highly engaged and fully behind your school vision, delivering their best every day, who want to stay with you for the long term. You'll have parents and a local community that work in partnership with your school and talk positively about it to others. They'll also know where to go for information, rather than chasing teachers for answers. And critically, it will result in students who are fully supported, giving them the best possible chance of being at their best and achieving great results.

Through the course of this book we'll take you through practical steps to develop your communication approach that will include:

- understanding how you are communicating today;

- knowing what could be holding you back;

- understanding your audiences, and knowing how best to communicate with each;

- achieving better communication outcomes;

- boosting your personal communication skills;

- communicating better with parents;

- working more effectively with your colleagues;

- using technology to your advantage; and

- checking how you are doing.

As a school leader, there are specific pointers to support you in being an inspirational communicator, attracting and retaining the best teachers and students, potentially enabling you to reduce your traditional marketing budget and ultimately achieving better academic results. These include:

- developing a meaningful vision, values and purpose;

- leading by example;

- using inspirational communication;

- creating an environment for entrepreneurial and innovative thinking; and

- managing school information.

This book has been aligned to the National Standards of Excellence for Headteachers (2015) to provide you with an 'inside out' approach to your school communication. So dive right in and start understanding how communication can make a difference to your school. In the first chapter we will look at what we mean by *communication* and why it is so important for your success. Good luck!

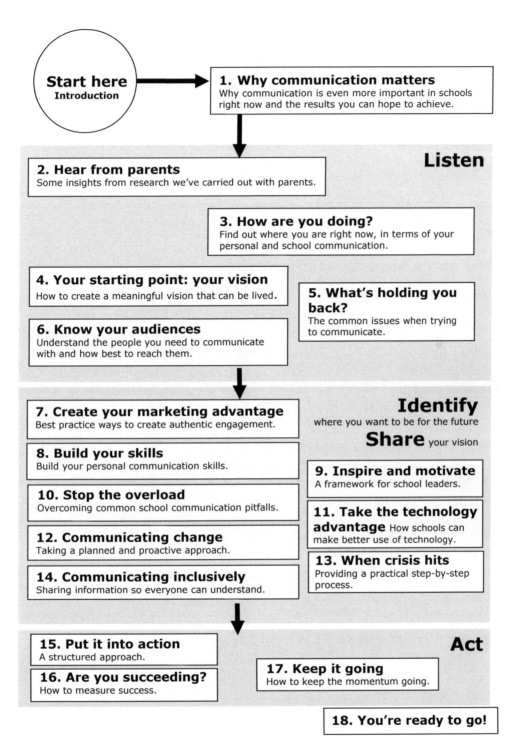

Figure 0.1 How to read this book

Communication matters

What do we mean by communication?

Communication is the art of listening, reading, observing and being self-aware, and then expressing thoughts or responding in speech, body language or writing.

In this first chapter we will look at what we mean by *communication* and why it is critically important for both you and your school. People often confuse information and communication. Information is only communication when it has been received and understood (in some sense) by the receiver. Good communication is when a message from the sender has been received and understood. This is the tricky part to get right, particularly with increased 'noise' that can cloud or even stop your message from getting through. Once you've read this book, you'll be in a much better position to ensure that you communicate well with each audience every time.

Everything you say and do is communication. You may have heard the statistics that only 7 per cent of communication is verbal. Ninety-three per cent is nonverbal – which means your body language and how you use your voice. Yet, few of us invest the time in making sure we have the right skills to communicate effectively. We take it for granted (because a lot happens in our subconscious), but there are many things you can do that will significantly enhance your ability to communicate more effectively.

Effective communication is critical

> *"The way we communicate with others and with ourselves ultimately determines the quality of our lives."*
>
> Tony Robbins

Whether in personal relationships or in the boardroom, communication creates better results in all walks of life. Big companies caught on to this opportunity some years ago. They know that if you communicate better as an organisation then you are more successful.

4

For example, in 2013, the *Harvard Business Review* carried out a survey to understand the impact of employee engagement (whether people are able to be at their best at work) on performance. They identified that **73 per cent of respondents ranked effective communication as a factor most likely to bring success** (only behind high level of customer service).

The Engage for Success report *The Evidence: Wellbeing and Engagement* (March 2014) highlighted that **organisations that have highly engaged employees are able to reduce staff turnover by 87 per cent**. In addition, disengaged employees are four times more likely to leave an organisation than the average employee (Corporate Leadership Council, 2008).

Companies with highly engaged staff report employees taking an average of 7 absence days per year, approximately half the 14 days per year reported in low-engagement companies. **Those employees in high-engagement companies also report significantly less workplace stress**, 28 per cent versus 39 per cent (Aon Hewitt, 2012).

It seems obvious and is proven, but schools still need to grasp this opportunity. Teachers need to be expert communicators to get the best out of the students they teach and to achieve great results. They need to have the ability to receive information holistically (what they hear and also what they don't hear), understand this and synthesize it so they can express themselves and respond really well. What they say needs to reflect their expertise, and inspire and demonstrate that they care about students, motivating them to want to learn.

School leaders in particular need to be able to inspire and motivate. This is something that is being reinforced by the Department for Education (DfE) through their National Standards of Excellence for Headteachers and is also an ongoing theme in Ofsted and Independent Schools Inspectorate (ISI) reports.

In schools that take the building of communication expertise seriously, teachers will be happier, which in turn will make for happier students who will achieve improved results. We all deliver more and better when we are happy and motivated. This 'discretionary effort' can make the difference between a good and outstanding school. And, of course, this all makes for happier parents who will also talk positively about the school.

I want to be at my best every day

We all want to be at our best every day. We want to thrive at work and believe in what we do. We want to be motivated to do our best and benefit ourselves and the school in which we work.

A lot of this comes down to a school's culture. James L. Heskett says that culture "can account for 20–30 per cent of the differential in performance when compared with 'culturally unremarkable' competitors."

Many organisations let their culture grow organically. However, a great culture should be purposeful and planned. **But what do we mean by *culture*?** It seems to have so many different aspects. John Coleman (2013) highlights six components of a great culture. These are:

1 **Vision:** Your culture starts with your vision.

2 **Values:** Values provide a guide on the behaviours and mindsets needed to achieve the vision.

3 **Practices:** Values need to be lived in the organisation's daily working practices.

4 **People:** Key to making this happen are the people who have shared values or want and are able to live the values.

5 **Narrative:** Every organisation has its own history and unique story. This narrative helps to create the culture.

6 **Place:** The place and environment in which the organisation operates that influences values and behaviours.

MacLeod and Clarke's *Concept of Employee Engagement* (2014) adds another enabler, which we believe is critical. This is integrity. Despite any of the above being in place, if leaders do not act with integrity then they mean very little.

The benefits of great communication

Great communication within your school will deliver very real and tangible benefits. Here are just some examples; there are many more **benefits you can hope to see if you improve how you communicate**:

1 You'll be able to better inspire and motivate your students to learn.

2 You'll be better equipped to respond to difficult and unexpected situations.

3 Parents and colleagues will understand what you are trying to say.

4 There will be less confusion and time wasted trying to address misunderstandings.

5 You'll take people with you on important decisions and ideas.

6 You'll be able to network better and share your views through social media.

7 You'll be more confident in communicating in front of larger audiences.

8 You'll be more aware of your own impact on other people.

9 More people will want to work with you.

10 Your relationships will be better (everywhere).

11 You'll be less stressed.

12 You'll grow in confidence and in your job.

13 Your students will benefit because you'll communicate better.

   If you invest time in understanding how to communicate better, you will be able to take further steps to be at your best. You will be able to help everyone else in the school be at theirs too. You will be able to build trust amongst teachers and parents. And you will develop a culture that everyone loves and can thrive in. In the next chapter we will look at feedback from parents about school communication and what they expect to see and hear from their school.

Top three take-aways:

1 Communication is everything you say and do.

2 Good communication skills are critical for every teacher and school leader.

3 If you improve communication, then you'll improve results.

2 Hear from the parents

Our independent research with parents across the UK, from both the state and private sector, highlighted communication as a fundamental issue for them. Parents want to be heard but don't always feel that there are ways for them to ask questions or give feedback. Parents rate communication from a school as a crucial factor in deciding where to send their child. The National Standards of Excellence for Headteachers (2015) call for positive relationships with parents, and yet our research shows that parents don't feel they have a voice and school communication needs to improve.

In this chapter we examine the relationship between how a school communicates and how parents feel about that school. It highlights what is important to parents regarding school communication and looks into the common issues that currently exist. While the feedback is both positive and negative, it is clear that at a time when expectations on both teachers and pupils are increasing, the opportunity to better engage parents in the educational process appears to be somewhat falling behind where it needs to be. Before we get into the details of the research, let's have a short summary of the history of parental involvement during the past 20 years.

Parental involvement – the history

In 1997, a Government White Paper titled *Excellence in Schools* described three ways in which to secure parent involvement. These were by providing parents with information, by giving them a voice and by encouraging parental partnerships with schools.

A 2003 research report by Professor Charles Desforges looking at, amongst other factors, the impact of parental involvement on pupil achievement following the Government's recommendations found evidence of a positive relationship between the two:

Parental involvement in the form of 'at-home good parenting' has a significant positive effect on children's achievement and adjustment even after all other factors shaping attainment have been taken out of the equation. … The scale of the impact is evident across all social classes and all ethnic groups.

(Desforges with Abouchaar, 2003)

Desforges also found that the extent and form of parental involvement was strongly influenced by family social class, that it diminishes as the child gets older and is strongly positively influenced by the child's level of attainment: the higher the level of attainment, the more parents get involved.

In 2010, the Department for Education's *Review of Best Practice in Parental Engagement* concluded that where schools had partnered with parents there were clear benefits:

Significant outcomes of parental support programmes include: parents acknowledging that a problem exists; gaining knowledge and skills to manage children's behaviour, and the confidence and empathy to use these skills effectively.

This same Department for Education review also outlined, however, some challenges to engaging with parents that are underlined by their ability to communicate well with them. For example, parents perceive schools as presenting obstacles to their engagement in the form of a lack of encouragement, not being clear about what they can do to support and being inflexible when it came to fitting around busy working and family lives. An increasing number of parents for whom English is not their first language, or those who have low levels of literacy and numeracy, were also less involved. It also requires commitment from the school and its leaders to maintain parentally focused activities, which for many were not sustainable.

We firmly believe that every child has the right to the best education possible with the right support from the right areas – importantly in their home life. Factors such as social class, language and attainment should not be barriers to children achieving their full potential.

Our research

In researching current levels of parental involvement and engagement for this book, we asked 100 parents from across the UK to respond to a number of questions that were designed to enable them to provide feedback on how well their school kept them informed. These questions are available in Appendix 2.1. A summary of our findings and their implications for parents are described in this chapter. We've also carried out further research directly with schools and these themes are consistent.

Information overload

Our research found that parents felt bombarded with information and were unclear as to what is important and what is just for information. Only 44 per cent of them felt well informed, 48 per cent said communication was okay and 8 per cent stated they were not well informed. This quote captures what many other parents expressed to us:

> *Send less frequent emails (I'm bombarded daily by 4–6 mails that can be a bit overwhelming) and make sure what you 'push' to me is important and relevant.*

The parent gap

Our research says that 94 per cent of parents stated how well a school communicates was an important factor in their choice of school. Parents want to help their children but aren't clear as to how they can complement what is done within the school or what 'good' looks like. They now make a more conscious choice about which school to send their children to. This comment from a parent summarises the direct link between meaningful communication and parental involvement:

> *I need to better understand what my child is being taught, and how we can assist in the learning process.*

One way only

Traditional one-way means of communicating and marketing are out of place in the modern world where everyone has a voice and information travels at lightening speed. Communication should be collaborative and involve a two-way exchange of dialogue. Our research found that 45 per cent of parents wanted more ways to ask questions and give feedback. Without this, parents are left feeling frustrated and that they don't have a voice within the school. A parent told us:

> *I want to be able to ask questions easily and discuss answers. Sometimes they may be simple questions that don't require a visit to school but I need to know where and who to ask.*

Teachers are not trained communicators

It may be surprising to some that in a career that is focused around being a good communicator, a robust communication-training programme is not a standard part of the teacher training process. Teachers need to be able to communicate well with parents, students and their colleagues to be successful. Our research found that 40 per cent of parents stated an area for improvement was teachers' ability to communicate.

The future is moving fast

Our research found that 30 per cent of parents wanted information faster and 38 per cent said schools should make better use of social media. A parent expressed these views nicely:

> *The schools should use social media to push information to me and allow me to ask questions, responding to queries quickly.*

Communication needs to be relevant

A view that came through strongly in the research and subsequently when we have spoken with other parents is they want and need communication to be targeted and much more specific to them and their child. School-wide and class-wide messages are fine up to a point, but schools need to also build a closer partnership at an individual level. For example, a parent told us:

> *I would prefer clearer child specific information about them more than twice a year in parents' evenings.*

Schools need to be more inclusive

As mentioned earlier in this chapter – schools need to work harder to reach all parents and not just those who are easy to reach because they are always there or speak a certain language:

> *Listen to everyone not just the mums (or dads) who help out at school.*

There were also some good experiences coming through in our research. A great example was:

> *The teacher emailed a weekly update to the parents of what the students did that week and what was expected the following week. Parents were also encouraged to email the teacher with questions or concerns, which also alleviated some of the congestion at school pick up time.*

It is not a coincidence that schools where parents are more engaged and involved in the school's activities are generally the ones producing the best academic results and have the happiest children. Parents have a unique ability and opportunity to influence at home behaviour, and to provide the relevant support for their child. Our research confirmed what we suspected and had also seen first-hand – school communication is inconsistent and *best practice* is not yet well defined nor followed.

This book aims to change that by defining best practice school communication for everyone. In the next chapter we will help you start that process by explaining how to understand your current starting point.

Top three take-aways:

1 Parental engagement is key to the success of students.

2 Parents want you to communicate with them and they want to have a conversation, not just information sent to them.

3 Parents want targeted, relevant and clearly signposted information that is easy to understand.

3 How are you doing?

In the previous chapter we shared the key findings of our independent research with parents that was carried out in the UK. It gives us a general view of what parents think about school communication. Now it's time to get specific and find out exactly how communication within your own school is working. This chapter will help you to work out your starting point.

An important first step is to understand how you are communicating at the moment. As you are likely to spend up to 80 per cent of your day either listening, speaking or communicating in some way, self-awareness can be very valuable and have a big impact on how well you do your job. It requires you to listen deeply with an open mind. You should also seek and listen to feedback from others on a regular basis about how you are communicating.

"We all need people who will give us feedback. That's how we improve."

Bill Gates

Consider these points when you seek feedback from others:

- **Be thankful** – Let people know that you appreciate it.

- **Actively listen** – Listen to what is said and learn to read between the lines (what isn't said but can be implied or seen in body language or tone).

- **It's nothing personal** – Don't take their comments personally or become defensive, however difficult that may be at times.

- **Make it real** – Seek to understand and absorb what they say. For example, ask for specific situations where you may have shown a particular behaviour.

- **Play it back** – Verbally summarise what you have heard to ensure you have understood correctly.

- **Keep to the facts** – Focus on the facts as much as possible and try to see beyond any emotional reactions.

If you respond well then others are more likely to feedback to you again, and be honest with you in the future.

It's important that you first understand how you are communicating, because:

- Your time is precious so any time you invest in improving your communication skills needs to be focused on where you can benefit most.

- It's easy to hear an isolated piece of feedback and react, but you need the full picture, in terms of how you are communicating.

- If you are thinking about investing in new communication technology or training, then pause. Check where the problem really is and ensure you invest wisely.

To this end, we've developed two sets of questions – one set is for you as a leader and the other is for your school. Answering the questions will produce a range of results that are aligned to the Ofsted rankings of Inadequate, Requires Improvement, Good and Outstanding. From this starting point you can identify areas you need to work on.

Your personal communication fitness test

To get an indication of your own communication fitness, complete the first test below and see how you score. For all questions, score yourself where 1 is the least favourable and 5 is the most. Please be honest (with yourself)!

1 How confident are you in your ability to communicate with students?

2 How well equipped are you to respond to difficult and unexpected situations with students?

3 Would your students say that their views are listened to?

4 How committed are you personally to improve your communication skills?

5 How well do you understand your school's vision or purpose?

6 How confident are you in communicating with parents?

7 Do you feel equipped to deal with difficult conversations with parents?

8 How confident are you in sharing your ideas with colleagues?

9 Do you feel equipped to influence others who have a different view to your own?

10 How often do you check if people have understood what you said?

11 How well do you believe you listen to others?

12 Are you clear on what you should and shouldn't say about your school on social media?

13 How confident are you in speaking to larger groups of people?

14 How strongly does your communication (written or spoken) reflect your school's purpose?

15 How clear are the messages you write or say to others?

16 How likely are you to experience misunderstandings and confusion when you communicate?

How did you score?

16–25 Inadequate

It might be time to build your communication skills. The good news is that you've made a start by being more self-aware. By making some simple changes, you'll see some real benefits and will be more fulfilled in your job. You've started to understand some of the areas where you are less confident. We'll guide you through how to improve in this book. So let's start the journey together.

26–45 Requires improvement

You are doing okay, but there is some room for improvement. There are simple things you can do to improve on the basics you have already. Think about where you felt least confident, and target these areas as you go through this book. Being self-aware is important, and you've taken a first step. Keep an eye and ear out for opportunities to understand more about how you are doing in your day-to-day job.

46–65 Good

You are doing well, and have a great foundation in place to build on. It won't take much for you to get to 'Outstanding'. Think about the areas where you felt less confident and keep them in mind as you go through this book. Actively ask for feedback from your peers to improve and continue to be self-aware.

66–80 Outstanding

You are doing very well, and are a communication role model! But remember that even the best of us have to keep improving. Ensure that you stay at the top of your game and continue to be the best by learning from some of the best practice in this book and asking for regular feedback from your peers.

Your school communication fitness test

Now, think about how your school is communicating overall. Again, for all questions, score your school where 1 is the least favourable and 5 is the most.

1 How well does everyone understand your school's common purpose?

2 To what extent are good teachers staying with your school?

3 To what extent are good teachers attracted to your school?

4 How positively is your school talked about on social media forums, local media and sites?

5 How strongly do all of your communication materials (newsletters, letters, printouts from your website, your prospectus) reflect your common purpose and reinforce your brand?

6 How clear is your school of the return on investment from your marketing or communication channel (text, email, intranet, website) spend?

7 How much time is invested in improving the communication skills of teachers?

8 How clear is day-to-day communication in terms of where to find information and what to do with it?

9 How easy is it for parents to share their views about your school?

10 To what extent would students say that their views are listened to?

11 How well informed are teachers about trends in education?

12 How well are your school leaders communicating, inspiring, motivating and listening?

13 How well do staff share their ideas and work together on issues to improve the school?

14 How well equipped are teachers with the tools and technology to communicate well with parents in your school?

How did your school score?

14–25 Inadequate
A score in this range indicates work to do within your school to get everybody aligned and on board with your common purpose. It is then necessary to communicate it well with all key stakeholders. Our best-practice guide will help you to put this all into action.

26–40 Requires improvement

You may have a common purpose in place, but more could be done to align teachers and parents behind it, to ensure that you are giving the best impression of your school at all times. Look for the gaps compared to our best-practice recommendations and aim to close them.

41–55 Good

You are clearly well aligned across all areas, and parents are generally positive about your school. If you are looking to become 'Outstanding', there are a few more steps to take.

56–70 Outstanding

Your school is doing very well, and is a role model for communicating and engaging key audiences. However, to ensure you stay where you are and continue to be a leading school, ensure you continue to follow best-practice guidelines.

It is important to become more self-aware, and you've accomplished that. Going through and answering these questions should have given you a better idea of where you are doing well and where you have areas for improvement. The questions are designed to ask you about areas that are key communication pain points and opportunities. As you move forward through the book, make sure you remember the areas that you have flagged up in this chapter and check back that you know where to focus your efforts. In the next chapter we explain how to start to build and develop your vision based on what you have just identified as your starting point.

Top three take-aways:

1 Self-awareness is key to being a great communicator.

2 Ask people for feedback and develop your ability to accept and learn from their comments.

3 However good you are at communicating, you can always improve.

4 Your starting point: Your vision

Before delving further into this book, it is important to understand your starting point in this journey. Your communication fitness test in the previous chapter should have given you a better idea of where you are right now. If you skipped that section, then go back and complete it, as it is crucial to the rest of the book. Once you know where you think you are, you can then find out what others might say about your school. This chapter takes you through the steps needed to develop a compelling and meaningful vision for your school. It explains how to ensure this vision is grounded and that it has real meaning for parents, teachers, students and governors. By the end of this chapter, you should be able to understand how to identify the gaps that exist between your vision and reality.

Listen and listen again

We call this the 'listen' phase in our model (Figure 4.1) for developing communication excellence.

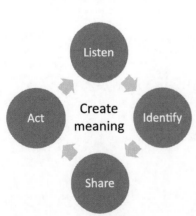

LISA

- **Listen** – a deeper listening to what the people most important to your school's success currently think, feel and do.

- **Identify** – where you want to be in the future. What will your school look, feel and sound like, and what will people think, feel and do in the future?

- **Share** – this first draft vision with those in your school. Build your vision together so you create a personal connection. Keep it simple and meaningful.

- **Act** – identify actions to get to your vision. These could be building communication skills (including your own), introducing a change in ways of working, creating understanding of your school's direction, enabling people to collaborate and connect and share best practice.

Figure 4.1 The LISA model

Start every conversation with a listening mindset, so you can find out what parents, governors, teachers and students believe you are doing well and what they think you could do better. As you have seen from our research, and as you are no doubt already aware, parents have strong views and are happy to share them when given the opportunity. So make sure that you ask! You can do this in a very manageable way without opening the floodgates, but it does require you to manage expectations about how you'll respond and take action.

Once you fully understand your starting point, you are in a position to develop and evolve the vision for your school that is the reference point for every communication that follows.

What is a vision statement and why is it important?

A *vision statement* is an aspirational description of what your school would like to achieve in the future. The National Standards state that school leaders should "communicate compellingly the school's vision and drive the strategic leadership, empowering all pupils and staff to excel." Ofsted inspectors measure how well the leaders' and governors' vision and ambition for the school are communicated to staff, parents and pupils.

This means that as a school leader you should understand and believe in your school's vision. It should state who you are as a school (your common purpose bringing together your promise to parents and children and your values) with an emphasis on what makes you different. It is what makes your school stand out from the crowd. No two schools are the same. They have different teachers, different students and different governors. However, how a school defines and crucially lives out its vision is what truly makes a difference. You want all of your parents to know what makes your school stand out. You need them to buy in to this 'unique differentiator' and to be advocates for your school when they talk to their friends.

Your vision should:

1 Be your North Star for everything

2 Be built by you and your team together

3 Be realistic as to where you are now

4 Be fit to support you in the future

5 Enable you to build your reputation

We look at each of these in more detail next.

Your North Star

Your vision should guide your current and future decisions and actions every single day. It is your North Star and the backbone to every decision, every policy and the people you recruit.

Amazingly, many organisations do not have a defined vision statement. Without a vision, any organisation will struggle to share its direction for the long term in a way that really creates a sense of unity. This common vision also enables a school to build a strong reputation. It is the backdrop to everything and contributes to a strong and positive reputation aligned to where your school is going.

Build it together

A vision should not be built by one person or in isolation by one group of people. It should have a level of ownership from all those who need to live it so it has real meaning and connects to both hearts and minds.

Make it realistic

You need to do your research to ensure it is realistic and you are not over promising. You need to be able to prove that you can deliver on your promise and have stories to bring this to life.

Make it future-proof

Think about the external environment and how education is changing, the changing expectations of parents, teachers and students and about where you want the school to be in five or ten years. What will it look, sound and feel like? Even with an already well-established vision statement, you still need to think about how your behaviours, processes and reward systems need to evolve as the external environment changes.

Build your brand and reputation

We've talked about this being your vision but you are actually starting to define your brand. Your brand is your reputation and this is everything to any organisation. A strong and positive reputation helps attract great teachers, creates a sense of a great learning environment and will result in loyal parents who talk positively about the school.

Do you have a vision already?

You may have a stated vision for your school that has been in place for many years. It was probably written with your school's motto in mind. But is it still relevant today? Does it reflect where your school is heading? Do people believe it and do you and your leadership team use it on a daily basis to guide your decisions? Are your behaviours, processes and reward systems aligned with it?

Do you need to develop a vision?

If you don't have a vision, you should still go through the same approach, listed below. You now have a clean slate to start with.

Seven steps to developing your vision

1 **Understand your strengths, weaknesses, opportunities and threats.**
   Take the Strengths, Weaknesses, Opportunities, Threats (SWOT) analysis test, using the template in Appendix 4.1, and list what you believe are your current strengths and weaknesses within your school and the opportunities and threats that exist in the external environment.

   Get together with the rest of your senior leadership team who have also gone through the SWOT analysis and share your observations. Are you all on the same page or are there big differences in how each of you sees your school's strengths, weaknesses, opportunities and threats? If there are differences, then now is the time to have an open and honest discussion with your team.

   When you have this conversation, try to go a little deeper than the average discussion, and imagine the future. What would it look and feel like? What would people be saying and doing? What would your leadership team like to leave behind when they move on?

2 **Build initial ideas for your vision from your SWOT insights.**
   Once you have shared views based on the SWOT analysis, write down key words from your brainstorm that you would like to capture and that you feel describe where you would like your school to be. This may be something completely new or an evolution of your existing vision.

   Ensure that every senior leader is able to contribute and that everyone gets to share their views. You will probably need to vote on your top key words that you would like in your vision. You then need to write down a first draft of your vision.

3 **Know what parents, teachers and students think.**

In parallel to the work you do with governors, you also need to understand the current perceptions of parents, teachers and ideally students. A simple question like, 'Which three words come to mind when you think about our school?' can help you to identify current perceptions.

There are some suggested survey templates that you could use to survey the parents of your students and some questions that you could ask your teachers and governors in Appendices 4.2 and 4.3.

4 **Know the reality of what people think externally.**

Your vision needs to be realistic and ensure you are not over promising based on external perceptions too.

This comes back to the listening part of the process we mentioned earlier. External listening could include monitoring traditional or social media, for example newspapers, magazines (online or printed) and channels such as Twitter or Facebook. Ideally you would actively listen into the media every day and there are organisations that can manage this for you. If, however, you would rather not invest in such services, you can still do a really great job of listening to social media at a fraction of the cost yourself.

To start with you should identify someone who can take responsibility and be the focal point for this. They could then use a free social media monitoring tool. Some popular ones at time of writing are HootSuite, Social Mention or Crowdfire. Use these to keep an eye on various social media sites, like Mumsnet, and see what is being said about your school. Get whoever is monitoring activity to build up a document that lists the types of words that are being used about your school, both positive and negative.

5 **Draw out insights from all of your research.**

Look at the key themes that come from this research and see how this fits with your vision:

- What are the key words that people use to describe your school?

- Are people talking about examples of where you are already living your vision? Can you reuse and share these stories more widely?

- Are there issues that need to be addressed to close the gap between reality and where you want to be?

- Are you standing out from the crowd for the right reasons?

- Are you seen to be living your values and leading by example?

Review the feedback that you have gathered and consider how this compares with your own perceptions. Were your views of what people thought of your school consistent with your own? Are there any areas more surprising than others that suggest things have worked better or worse than you had anticipated?

6 **Develop your vision in a way that has meaning.**
Now that you have some great input and insights, it is time to develop your draft vision. Avoid technical jargon or textbook language. Write it how you would tell someone who knows nothing about education and nothing about your school. Ensure it is succinct and is immediately understandable by children and adults alike. Make it appealing, and try to connect at an emotional level.

Most people will focus on the 'what' – we educate and inspire children. Or maybe even the 'how' – through the best teachers and facilities. But the best way to focus people and grab their attention is to define the 'why'. Why does your school do what it does and why does that matter? For example, 'We are creating a generation that can give something back to the world' is slightly more compelling and connects better with people's emotions than 'We deliver great education'.

7 **Test your vision.**
The best way to sense check your draft vision statement is with the rest of the teaching team, governors and even students, although maybe not all at the same time! Think about using representatives of each of these groups as part of the development team.

Bring them together in a friendly environment to gather their views. Does it resonate with them? Does it make them feel proud? Do they think it makes your school stand out from the crowd? Ensure you make this a comfortable and open conversation where there are no wrong answers.

This is a critical step. This group of people must believe in and live your vision every day for it to have meaning and come to life. Your vision should be long lasting so it's really worth putting this time in to get it right.

Ready for the next stage

After developing your vision and sense checking it with your internal and external stakeholders, you now have a starting point for your action plan. It is important your vision is lived every day by every member of your teaching staff. In the next chapter, we look at what might be holding you back from making your vision a reality and actions that you can take to overcome this.

Top three take-aways:

1 Listening is key to understanding where you are right now.

2 Build your vision together with your team.

3 Create a vision that has real meaning for all school audiences.

5 What is holding you back?

In the previous chapter, we talked about developing the vision for your school. Now, you have great intentions to improve communication as part of that vision. Perhaps you have tried things that aren't working, or you just can't find the time to invest in making changes. Or maybe you've tried ad hoc initiatives, like introducing a new website, and you don't even know if they've made a difference. In this chapter, we look at what could be holding you back from being successful, in terms of communication. Once you know your obstacles, you can take action to address these issues and move forward. The issues that you face will be common across many schools, so by addressing them you will be able to get ahead of others and unlock the power of communication to drive success.

We don't have the time

We know that everyone in schools is busy. In fact, many teachers and school leaders are overloaded to the point of extreme stress. We've already covered *why* communication will enable you to be successful. However, should you need a little more persuasion to invest time, then think about the following scenario.

We know that parents want to ask questions, and often have relevant and timely information about their children's education. Generally, schools expect parents to go to their website or pick up emails and texts. Sadly, this expectation isn't communicated or delivered very well in many cases. As a result, parents are not clear on who they should speak to or when, so they reach out to the most visible point of contact – the teachers. Now, if you had invested in a planned and structured approach to communication, parents would know where to go for key information and they would be confident they will receive what is relevant to them in a timely manner. Their expectations would be managed, and they would understand that they should only go to teachers directly in specific circumstances. Teachers could then concentrate on teaching rather than answering unnecessary emails. It would save everyone a lot of time.

We don't need a communication plan – we already invest in marketing

School communication budgets are often focused on external marketing activities, such as advertising, websites, sponsorship or events. These do not support the fundamental foundation of how people communicate within the school.

This includes:

- Communication within the school between teachers

- School leaders' ability to motivate and inspire their school team

- Making teachers better communicators

- Enabling teachers to communicate well with parents

- Providing information to support parents in playing their part in their children's education

- Giving students, teachers and parents a voice when they have great ideas to improve a school

- Enabling teachers, parents and students to be advocates for the school

- Ensuring information is well managed and completely aligned to the school vision

We will talk about how to develop your communication plan later in the book. Essentially, the plan should cover everyone you wish to communicate with – those inside the school, such as your teachers, and those outside, such as parents. It is also worth remembering that, generally, what you say to your internal audiences will quickly be heard out beyond the walls of your school. This is because the growth and ease of access of social media has made this an instant process available to anyone, turning the traditional news coverage model on its head. In fact, it is estimated that in the UK alone, every single statement posted online will reach at least 250 people. If you understand the communication issues and opportunities for your school, then you can focus your limited resources on the ones that impact you and where you'll receive the greatest return on investment.

Without a proper plan you may carry out one off and ad hoc activities that won't be focused in the right direction and you won't see the benefit. Instead, by having a clear set of communication goals, as part of your plan, to address real problems, and by delivering a set of activities over the short, medium and long term, you'll see the results you need to be on your journey to outstanding communication.

Common communication issues that hold schools back

Based on our research, we know that there are consistent factors related to communication that schools aren't getting right. They include:

1 Information overload

2 The parent–school partnership gap

3 No trained communication-specialist resource

4 People aren't aware of the impact of their personal communication style

5 One-way communication isn't enough

6 The future is moving fast – schools need to catch up

We look at each of these issues in more detail here.

Information overload

Information is everywhere. There is more information available today, more ways to find information, and more ways for companies to contact us than ever before. It's not just traditional post, television and radio channels, but through the Internet on almost every site we visit, through our social media activities, our emails and texts. Parents of school-age children have all of this plus the information their child's school sends to them. It is no surprise they feel bombarded with information and are unclear as to what is important and what is just for information. Which one of the 200 messages they have received today do they read first and how does a school make sure it is their message that stands out from the others in the crowd?

The parent–school partnership gap

Parents want to help their children, but are not clear as to how they can complement what is done within the school or what 'good' looks like. They now make a more conscious choice where to school their children and some of that is based on how well a school communicates with them. We also know that parents' expectations are not being managed in terms of their role in their children's education due to missed communication at the outset of the relationship between the school and parents. This often creates a perception from parents that they don't have a role to play and can leave education up to the school, with little intervention or support. For those who do have a home–school partnership or similar in place, it's often not referred back to on an ongoing basis so becomes a distant memory, when it could be drawn upon regularly to achieve better student outcomes.

Listening is also key in your relationship with parents and is something that isn't always done well. We don't just mean to ask them to email you if they have concerns or questions. Listening should be something schools become masterful in so they can understand the real issues in a systematic way. By putting a framework in place to proactively listen to parents, you'll benefit because you'll be able to make improvements where they matter most, and parents will greatly value that you are listening.

No trained communication-specialist resource

Teachers are not experts in managing communication as a process. They also don't formally receive training in how to communicate with parents. This means there is generally no one in a school who is able to 'double-hat' and support great communication within that school. Often, the responsibility for communication is given to an assistant, who is unlikely to be an expert in both communication skills and processes.

People aren't aware of the impact of their personal communication style

As teachers and school leaders do not receive formal communication training as part of their teaching qualification, they are not always aware of how much their personal communication style and actions impact every interaction. These interactions could be with parents, their fellow teachers or students. A poor communication experience is often talked about and rapidly impacts the reputation of the school. There also needs to be a real understanding of what parents and the local community think about the school so perceptions can be managed with facts.

One-way communication isn't enough

Quality communication should generally be collaborative and involve a two-way exchange of dialogue (i.e. a conversation). Without this, information can be misunderstood – you don't know what has been communicated, you may miss out on great ideas and/or feedback and people can feel frustrated that they don't have a voice or anyone to ask questions of. This two-way process can also apply to students. Their voices needs to be heard, especially in a world where having a voice is increasingly the norm.

The future is moving fast

Traditional one-way communication and marketing are out of place in the modern world, where everyone has a voice and the ability to send and receive information with a click of the keyboard. Education is traditionally slow to adopt new thinking, which is reflected in the approach to communicating with parents and students through channels such as a printed prospectus, static websites and letters in school bags.

We've already mentioned listening in relation to parents, and to do this well you need to rethink how you communicate, beyond one-way communication. It's crucial to not only listen to parents but also to teachers, students and the local community.

Social media has opened up new opportunities. Along with other technology, these media provide many alternative options to actual face-to-face communication – en masse and across geographical boundaries, employing such technological strategies as webcasts, Skype or live video.

This chapter should have aided in a better understanding of what might be hindering you from turning your vision for your school into reality through great communication. Now we move forward and address some of these challenges. In the next chapter, we explain how to better understand those you communicate with most so that you can make every communication meaningful to them every time.

Top three take-aways:

1 Invest time in managing communication proactively to gain real results and better student outcomes.

2 Be aware of common factors that could be holding your school back from outstanding communication.

3 Invest time and money where you know you have a real issue and then focus on it in a planned and sustained way.

Case study: Visionary leadership delivers results

In the example of St Michael's school, Bowthorpe, Tony Hull (Headteacher) has been awarded for his "razor-sharp vision and clarity of thought". His introduction of a new tier of management turned around a violent school that had lost its way. School inspectors praised this as one of the most 'dynamic' management teams they had ever seen. And this is not his only success story. In the last 10 years, Tony Hull has helped three Norwich primary schools – St Michael's in Bowthorpe, Norwich, Costessey juniors and West Earlham juniors – out of special measures and put them on a stronger footing.

6 Know your audiences

In the previous chapter, we talked about what might be holding you back from effective communication. One of the most important aspects of communication is knowing the people you are aiming your message towards. This is often called the *target audience*. If you don't know who they are, their motivations and what they currently think, then you won't be able to deliver a message that resonates with them. It is important to ensure there is a clear 'what's in it for me' element for people to take notice, particularly in the midst of the noise and speed of information in today's world. You need to be clear about what you want people to know, feel and do as a result of any communication. This applies to all communication, whether it is a written message or verbal communication. The thought process should be the same.

This chapter provides a framework for determining who the most important audiences are and where to focus your efforts. It also reminds you to look beyond the most obvious audiences, to those where there is real value for your school.

Identify who influences your school's success

To understand your most powerful audiences, you need to identify who will have the greatest influence on the success of your school. This does not mean you ignore everybody else; you need to communicate with all your audiences appropriately. However, knowing who your primary influential groups are will enable you to focus your energy and resources where they will have the greatest impact. You then need to understand their unique needs, where they are now and where you want them to be to ensure they are advocates for your school.

List your audiences

Firstly, list all your potential audiences. They may include parents, teachers, the parent–teacher association, students, the Board of Governors, your leadership team, the cleaners, the reception/school office staff, local MPs, the people who work in

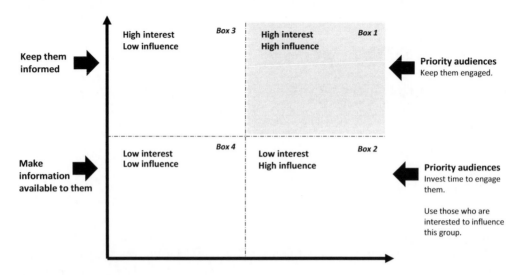

Figure 6.1 Understanding your audiences

the canteen or the sports ground or maintenance people. All of these people can be potential influencers. Remember that one message can reach 250 people, no matter where it comes from.

Once you've determined your audiences, plot each one on a simple grid, as shown in Figure 6.1. Determine each audience-group's level of interest (or engagement) in your school and the level of influence it has.

Those with **high interest** and **high influence** [Box 1] are your priority audience. They are highly interested in the success of your school, and have the most influence on this. Typical groups in here would be governors, teachers, academy chain leaders or parent representatives. This is where you will need to focus your efforts and be very open, using lots of two-way communication.

Those with **high influence** and **low interest** [Box 2] need to also be kept informed, but in a very different manner, recognising their lower interest levels. They may not even be aware of their influence, so they need to be managed carefully. Typical groups in here would be other local schools or the local media.

Those with **high interest** but **low influence** [Box 3] need to be kept well informed by regular communication that is targeted specifically for them. Typical groups in here would be students.

The final group with **low interest** and **low influence** [Box 4] need to know where to go to find information and can be included in any general communication. Sadly, some parents may fall in here although your aim would be to raise their interest levels and move them into Box 3.

A completed version could look like the example in Figure 6.2:

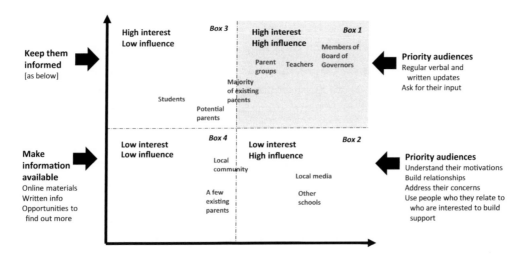

This picture will alter according to specific changes. For example, you will see an increased level of local community interest if you are expanding your school and seeking planning permission.

Figure 6.2   Understanding your audiences: an example

Understand their unique needs

Try to 'step into the shoes' of your priority audiences and understand their unique needs, including where they may be and where you need them to be in order to create advocates. Think about how you will communicate well with them depending on their unique needs. For example, looking at the teachers in your school, think firstly about simple demographics such as the average length of employment, their interests and job role. This will give them a unique 'filter' with which they see the world and hear what you have to say. Teachers with longer service might be more resistant to new ways of doing things compared to newly qualified teachers or those in their early years of teaching.

Then think about the types of people that you are communicating with. For example, they will all have a preference for how they communicate, whether that is visual, auditory or kinaesthetic, otherwise known as seeing, listening or feeling. People use all three styles to receive and learn new information and experiences. However, one or two of these receiving styles is normally dominant. This dominant style defines the best way for a person to learn new information by filtering what is to be learned. You therefore need to decide when to present information using all three styles and when to use just one or two depending on your audience.

You will also have some people who prefer to have information and formulate their thoughts before they are 'put on the spot' to share their views, whereas others may be more comfortable thinking on their feet. You'll need to develop approaches that work across all areas. You may find that you have a lot of younger teaching staff that you need to communicate with differently. They are likely to expect more online and instant communication and be looking at progressive education techniques.

When looking at parents, on average how many children do they have at the school? Where do children come from and go to after your school? Where do parents live and what is the socioeconomic background? Are there lots of working parents, for example, who need communication they can easily access during their working day?

You should also consider the demographic of your audience. If you are in an under privileged area where some homes do not have home computers and Internet access, putting everything online may not be the best approach. If you are in an area where there are a lot of students for whom English is a foreign language and their parents do not speak English, providing them with clearly written information is important or the opportunity of translated information.

Understand how far you need to move your audiences' mindsets

You can now put yourself in the shoes of your audiences. Imagine what they currently think, feel and do in relation to the subject you need to communicate. Where do you need them to be after you communicate? What is the gap you need to close? See the template in Appendix 6.1 to support you in thinking this through for each audience.

Know the best communication channel for your audience and outcome

The importance of assessing your available communication channels and your various audiences cannot be overstated. Table 6.1 shows a breakdown of communication channels and how they can work best for different types of people and audiences.

You should now be clear about exactly who you need to communicate with, and why, based on their levels of interest and influence. You will be clear on who your priority audiences are and how to reach them. In the next chapter we will explain how to create your own marketing advantage by using what you now know about your most important audiences.

Table 6.1 Choose the right channel to achieve your communication outcome

How to use this matrix: Take a look at each channel and review what is good and not good about each to see which best fits your communication outcome. Watch out for those pitfalls.

Channel type	Example	Good for	Not good for	Avoid the pitfalls
Face-to-face	• Parent–teacher conference or meetings. • Parent forums. • School events like open days or sports day.	• Motivating and energising people. • Building trust and advocacy. • Sensitive or very important information. • Encouraging feedback and ideas. • Sharing visual and 'real' stories from students.	• Pure information sharing where it requires no explanation.	• Don't talk at people – make it a conversation. • Prepare your communication and practice extensively to make the most of the opportunity. • Don't have too many face-to-face events, especially at times when parents can't attend.
Internet	• School website. • Virtual learning environment. • Online parent and homework sites. • Teacher–student online areas. • Video/audio.	• Providing core school information. • Supporting the parent–school partnership, i.e. homework can be accessed online. • Humanise stories about your school and the headteacher/ teachers through videos.	• Sensitive information • Information that requires explanation or is lengthy.	• Have an integrated external/internal online platform to automate things like permission forms. This will create a great experience for all in your school, and demonstrates you are delivering on modern communication needs.
Paper based	• Prospectus. • Newsletter. • School letters.	• Providing core information about your school and supporting images. • Reinforce your vision and provide regular student stories. • Letters for parents' attention.	• Prospectuses and newsletters are not good for time-sensitive or urgent information. They aren't good for sensitive information that requires explanation. • Letters are not always great for urgent and important information, as they get lost and don't always make home.	• Avoid heavy prospectus, which are costly and where you are not clear on the return on investment. • Instead, focus on online materials with one-page printouts so parents can print just what they need when they want it. This includes paper letters and forms, which could instead be completed online. • Not everyone wants an online newsletter. Provide the option of a low-cost paper-based newsletter. This can actually be beneficial in creating a third-party endorsement for your school when sat on a parent's coffee table.

Table 6.1 continued

Channel type	Example	Good for	Not good for	Avoid the pitfalls
Email	• To and from teachers. • Weekly email newsletters. • Year/class/school emails to parents.	• Contacting teachers/school/ parents on important topics in a targeted and personalised way. • Relatively time-sensitive information and where you need to know people have received it (return receipts).	• Too regular information (overload). • Information that is not clearly targeted or focused, i.e. it's not clear what people should do with it. • Information that needs explanation or discussion.	• Our research shows that email can be feast or famine. Don't bombard people, but use it well, making it clear whether something is for action or for info – possibly using a traffic-light system, with red being the most important.
Text	• Text messages in emergencies. • Reminder text messages.	• Time-sensitive updates or alerts. • Short messages.	• Information that needs explanation or discussion. • Lengthy information. • Sensitive information.	• Like email, text messages can be under or over done. Don't bombard people, and use them only when you really need to alert people or they can lose their value and will be ignored.
Apps	• Core school information. • Discussion forum. • Homework information. • School calendar. • Alerts. • Newsletters. • Contact information.	• Bringing together all useful school information onto a device that most parents use on a daily basis. • Creates a 'self-service' and modern technology approach.	• Information that needs explanation or discussion. • Lengthy information. • Sensitive information.	• These can be expensive to produce so ensure you are going to invest the time in making it work for your school.
Social media	• Facebook or Twitter presence. • Discussion forums.	• Promoting stories about the school. • Engaging in discussion. • Sharing viewpoints.	• Sensitive information. • Information that requires explanation or is lengthy.	• Have one person who monitors your social media channels so you can be proactive in managing your online reputation.

Advertising/ sponsorship	• Open day and general school promotion.	• Information that needs explanation or discussion. • Lengthy information. • Sensitive information.	• Are you achieving return on investment on your advertising or sponsorship? Instead, you could focus your energy on social media and building parent advocates. This will deliver a good result at a lower cost.
	• Short, targeted promotional messages and supporting images.		
Media	• Stories in magazines and newspapers or on the radio or TV.	• Information that needs explanation or discussion. • Lengthy information. • Sensitive information.	• Build relationships with local media both to share stories but importantly to build trust in case things go wrong and you need help in managing your reputation.
	• Short, targeted promotional messages and supporting images to build thought leadership and raise the profile of the school through student stories.		
Surveys	• Quick polls. • Questionnaires.	• Information that needs explanation or discussion. • Lengthy information. • Sensitive information.	• Gathering ideas, feedback and understanding viewpoints.
			• Two-way communication is vital so it's important to show you are listening. But if you invite feedback ensure you demonstrate that you have responded and taken action where you can. Otherwise people are less likely to respond in the future.

Top three take-aways:

1 Identify your key audiences who have the greatest influence and interest in your school.

2 Understand what is important to each audience.

3 Communicate with them in ways that work best for them, not just for you.

Create your own marketing advantage

There is increased pressure on schools to deliver better results year on year. This means there is natural competition between schools to attract the best teachers and high-performing pupils. Marketing a school authentically, to attract such teachers and students, through traditional marketing channels, is challenging and can be costly.

While shiny brochures and flashy websites look great, they are not very authentic. Every brochure or website has a photo of smiling children and happy teachers and many of them even have similar words. However, as discussed earlier in this book, that does not reflect the reality at their school. People today are very quick to search for reviews before they buy a new product. Parents are no different when it comes to researching prospective schools for their children. They will look for reviews online, look at the Ofsted report and ask their friends who may have children at the school. It is extremely likely they will find both good and bad reviews to help them make up their minds.

If all of the good reviews are through the traditional marketing channels and the bad reviews are from other parents, it will almost certainly lead them to believe the worst. As a result, schools need to look for new opportunities to promote themselves through more authentic means. In this chapter we look at how to use the knowledge you now have about your most influential audiences to create your own marketing advantage.

Getting the balance right

Achieving the right balance means investing equally between what could be called 'internal marketing' and more traditional 'external marketing'. If you imagine internal and external marketing and communication investment as two sides of a set of scales, they need to be balanced. If you put too much weight on one side, they won't balance (see Figure 7.1).

Practically speaking, this means that if you spend lots of time and money on building your profile externally but fail to spend equal measure ensuring your

Where are you focusing your time?
The critical balance between internal and external communication

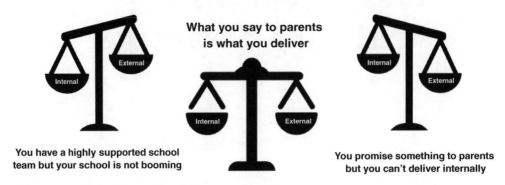

Figure 7.1 Scales of marketing balance

teachers and staff understand their roles and what your vision means to them, they would not be in a position to advocate for your school when the additional enquiries start to come in. This would potentially mean the end result is worse than if you had done nothing as potential parents' expectations will have been lifted and then crashed.

On the other hand, over-investing internally means you have an amazingly motivated and engaged team, but potential parents don't get to hear about them, as your marketing spending is too low. Getting the balance right is crucial.

Be authentic

Firstly, your school needs to develop the messages that it wants people to hear based on your vision. You should define, sitting with your team, what you want your school to be known for – its common purpose or vision. By building this with the teachers and others involved with your school, you will create something they believe in and can easily share. Once they can easily share what the school is about, they are in a stronger position to become an advocate for your school, whether they are speaking with a parent, talking at a meeting or interacting online.

Benefit from social media

As mentioned earlier in the book, your school may be nervous about school employees speaking about your school on social media channels. But if you agree on and share some clear ground rules, then using social media can be a very powerful tool. To start with, develop some social media guidelines that make it very clear what can and cannot be said online about the school. These should cover what is said in an official formal school capacity and what is shared personally. (A draft of a sample social media policy can be found in Appendix 7.1.)

The real power of social media is the ability to reach lots of people quickly. It is estimated that on average any individual in the UK has the ability to interact with around 250 people at any one time (2016 Digital Yearbook). This could be through friends and family and social media connections. So if you imagine that just ten employees were speaking positively about your school, they have the potential to reach at least 2,500 people very quickly. This is far more than could be achieved through traditional marketing techniques.

But employees speaking positively about their employer isn't really that groundbreaking or even compelling. Yes, they are giving a positive view, but they are also paid employees so may be expected to do so to a certain extent. So, imagine if you were able to turn existing parents into advocates? These are your customers and everyone knows that customers tell it like it is. If you communicate consistent messages about your school to parents, listen to their feedback, take actions where you can and explain when you can't, you will develop a group of parents that are much more likely to talk positively about your school to others. When you take into account their 250 connections each it is clear how powerful an engaged group of parents could be through social media. So rather than be fearful of social media, embrace it and find ways to encourage parents to start up discussions with other parents on relevant topics.

Build your reputation through the media

Many schools issue media releases about the latest sports win or academic success, but, despite creating some goodwill, this tends to be a reactive approach. Just think if you adopted a focused and proactive media approach that positioned your school as a thought-leader in certain topics.

For example, if your school vision talks about diversity, you could talk broadly about how you are encouraging that within your school and what actions children and others are taking. The media can be a very powerful way to raise your profile if you can identify a few things that make your school stand out from the crowd.

If you are able to build relationships with journalists and online publications, then you will have more chance of receiving coverage. Provide them with regular and relevant content they can use. As a school leader, there is an opportunity to position yourself and relevant teaching staff as thought-leaders in your key topics or new fields for teaching.

Ensure that you share any media releases with your own school employees at the same time as issuing them externally. This avoids any surprises; for example, if a teacher is approached by a journalist, he or she will be prepared. You clearly want your staff to be able to redirect the enquiry correctly and respond appropriately.

Other ways to receive coverage are through past pupils highlighting their achievements and stories. You can also do something called *piggybacking*, where you see a topic in the media and recognize you have an expert on the topic or are doing it particularly well. You can 'jump on the back' of this coverage and contact relevant journalists who are already interested in the topic. You should use your website to link to any online coverage you receive, and make sure that you share it with parents and within the school.

Use your website in new ways

In our research we found that parents feel that school websites often fall very short of their expectations. However, many schools invest a lot of money into re-developing them without really thinking about what people need and the opportunities to use them well.

We firstly recommend that you understand what is working well and what is not with your website before investing any further. But there are ways to maximise how you use your website beyond the traditional marketing approach of text and photos:

- **Use videos of children and parents** talking about their experience of your school and what they like most about the school.

- **Show school leadership through video.** Replace the rather long and outdated headteacher's welcome letter with a shorter message and accompanying video so people have a greater sense of the type of person who is leading the school.

- **Make your website easier to read.** Cut back on the amount of text on your website. Writing for the web requires a different style to other written communication. People want succinct information and to see photographs.

- **Create the opportunity for two-way communication.** Include quick polls to gather quick temperature checks on issues where you would like input (and where parents need to be heard).

- **Is your website intuitive?** Can people find the information they need easily and quickly? Any more than two clicks away is often too much.

- **One place for parent, teacher and student information needs.** Integrate your website with core information with an online learning environment and parent community site. You can also have an area which is just for teachers so they can share ideas and also post to the site directly. Ensure that you have guidelines in place to manage this approach well.

You can also use tried-and-tested apps (applications). Take a look at something like Schoop to enable parent–school communication through a reliable and modern technology platform.

Rethink your open days

Open days tend to follow a similar formula, and generally parents will attend more than one to understand the options of schools available to them. If you follow exactly the same formula as everyone else, then you won't stand out from the crowd. Here are some tips:

- Send out a **welcoming video/email** to those attendees a couple of days before the open day. This could be a message from the students, teachers and headteacher saying how much they are looking forward to seeing new parents and children.

- **Don't overload people with paper** as soon as they get there. Give them something to read or watch if they are waiting for a talk or the like, but don't overload them. Consider following up after the event with links to online materials and a thank-you message.

- If you have a formal talk at the start, then minimise the time that the headteacher and other senior teachers speak. When they do speak ensure they are as engaging and inspiring as possible. Use personal stories, drawing out what makes your school different, rather than saying the same as every other school. If there are children in the audience, make it inspiring for them too. **Focus more time on involving your school's students in the talk,** or even have current parents with them talking about their experience of your school.

- It's great to have students take prospective parents and children around the school, but when children go to the classrooms, ensure there are **practical and fun things for them to do, to demonstrate your school's teaching ability.** Clearly you want children to be asking their parents if they can go to your school over any other school.

- **Ask attendees how the open day went** so you can learn and improve. This can be a paper-based survey or an electronic version (through something like Survey Monkey) emailed after the event, together with a thank-you-for-attending message. Keep it short and specific to what you wanted the open day to achieve, and provide opportunity for open comments.

Involve your students

You could ask your students to form an editorial team and be the journalists for your school, searching out good and bad stories to share and report on. These could then be shared in your school newsletter or at open days and other events where parents gather together.

Marketing from the inside out

The power of authentic advocacy far outweighs any other form of marketing. Ensuring that you are marketing your school from the inside out is absolutely critical to your success. It may also save you some money! If you aim to communicate well with those who carry the most influence for your school, then you are likely to gain the best-value return for your time invested. In the next chapter, we discuss your personal communication role as a leader of the school to ensure that the school has a motivated, respected and effective teaching staff to deliver a high-quality education for all pupils.

Top three take-aways:

1 Build loyalty and advocacy from the inside out.

2 Seek out alternatives to traditional marketing channels.

3 Use the power of social media to market your school.

Build your skills

8

Everyone should regularly invest in building their communication skills. But actually how much time should you invest in this important development that impacts around 80 per cent of what you do in your job? It's easy to take it for granted, to let it drop down the list of priorities and leave it to chance. Sadly, poor communication causes confusion and damages reputations, both your own and that of your school, so it is worth the investment. Up until now we have focused on communication from your school and how to get that right. In the next two chapters, we look at your own skills as a leader of your school. We will take you through simple and practical steps so you can proactively and continually improve your communication skills. We review the following areas:

1 Understanding your personal communication style

2 Knowing how you are communicating

3 Developing a communication mindset

4 Knowing how to actively listen

5 Generating ideas to make your communication even more effective

6 Managing more challenging communication

Understanding your personal communication style

Although most of us think we communicate well, we can always improve. Through improving your communication skills, you will achieve more in your day-to-day work. You'll have less confusion, better results and you'll be more fulfilled in your role (and a lot less frustrated). This is important in your interactions with parents, your team members and students.

Firstly, let's remind ourselves of what is basic communication at a personal level. In its simplest form, communication is a process between at least two people, where one person wants to communicate with the other. The person who wants to communicate is the sender and the person who will receive the communication is the receiver. The sender may want to communicate feelings, images, words or thoughts. The receiver will have many different preconceptions or perspectives. They will experience the world through their own life lens and not that of the sender. Therefore, how they receive what the sender wants to communicate will be translated in different ways.

In today's connected world, communication is rarely a linear process. There are usually many other things going on at the same time and we rarely give our full attention to communicating with one person at a time.

People will also have different preferences for how they both want to communicate and how they want to be communicated with. Introversion and extroversion are two extremes of preferences that describe where people get their energy from. Introverts take their energy from within and extroverts from their external environment. This has an impact on how these types like to give and receive communication. Extroverts can typically speak more freely and answer instantly whereas introverts are often more thoughtful in their approach and prefer to have thinking time to respond. To get the best out of people, it is important to understand them fully and slightly adapt your style for the best outcome.

So personal communication is full of potential pitfalls, in terms of opportunities to make mistakes.

Knowing how you are communicating

The first step is to understand how well you are doing at the moment. If you haven't already, then take the short test at the start of this book (Chapter 3) to understand your starting point. Better still; gather feedback from your colleagues about what you do well and what you could do better. Next, think about areas to focus on. Consider whether you have developed a communication mindset, and if there are aspects that you can improve.

Developing a communication mindset

It's not always possible to plan every communication, but where you can, then think about the following to give you clarity of thought:

a What is your outcome?
What do you need to achieve through this communication? For example, what is the problem you want to overcome or what is the change that you want to take place? Imagine what it would look like when you get there and what you want people to think, feel and do.

b Understand your audience

Who are your most important audiences (who you need to communicate with) and what do they currently think, feel and do? We covered how to analyse your audiences in Chapter 6 so if necessary go back and remind yourself of this first. As the saying goes, it is important to seek first to understand before you try to be understood. This means taking the time to see other people's perspectives by asking the right questions. Listen fully to what they say. (See the discussion later in this chapter for guidance on how to listen actively.)

Consider this even more if someone is from a different culture, as this will impact the communication. Think about how your audience likes to take on information – some will be visual, some auditory and some kinaesthetic (feeling). Listen to the words they use to recognise these different communication types. For example, they may say 'I see your point', or 'I hear what you are saying' and 'I've got a feel for where you are going'.

In addition, you'll have people who prefer to absorb information and then respond (introverts) and those who are able to digest it quickly and give an on the spot response (extroverts). One option is to share information before your event or meeting to allow people to digest the information ahead of time to ensure you achieve the widest possible engagement and input.

c Understand how communication can help

Pay attention to understanding the gap, if there is one, and think about some ways you may go about closing the gap between where people are at the moment and where you need them to be. It could be a simple face-to-face discussion in the right environment or it might need to be a broader or formal communication, such as an email or meeting.

d Develop your message

You should have no more than three key points. Ensure these are clear in your mind. Think about what the audience may already know and think about what you want them to know, feel and do as a result of your communication.

e Use the right communication method

It's important to use the right communication approach for different information. For example, sensitive information, such as letting someone know his or her role is being made redundant, should be handled face to face. On the other hand, make sure to use the right method when sharing good news. For example, if someone in your team has won an award, don't just bury it in a circular email, but make a point of sharing the news in person with colleagues to create both recognition and a sense of achievement for everyone.

If you are writing an email, then keep it to the point and ensure you proofread it well. Make the title/subject clear, including what you want done as a result. Include a deadline if there is one. Don't rely on email for important information. Follow it up with a phone call wherever possible.

If you are at an event and you really have to use slides, then don't put lots of words on each one. Keep slides to an absolute minimum, because people can't read at the same time as they listen. If they have to read lots of text, then they won't be listening to what you say.

The slides can have a single bold fact or figure, giving people time to read and digest it, or also include an image that illustrates and strengthens the point. Pictures along with words on a slide make a bigger impact.

The work of Edgar Dale and his cone of learning (1969) to inform how you communicate identified that we remember:

- 10 per cent of what we read

- 20 per cent of what we hear

- 30 per cent of what we see

- 50 per cent of what we see and hear

- 70 per cent of what we discuss with others

- 80 per cent of what we personally experience

- 95 per cent or what we teach others

f   Communicate and make sure you've been successful

Crucially you now need to deliver your message to achieve your outcome. Check if you have been successful by clarifying what people have heard and what they now think, feel and have done or will do (your outcome).

Knowing how to actively listen

We talk a lot throughout this book about listening because it is so fundamental to communication and our lives. Sometimes we take it for granted that people know how to listen well. But we've all experienced situations in which we know people are not listening, even though they may be physically in front of us.

So what does good listening look like and how can you listen better? Take a look at the following points to learn more:

Understand passive versus active listening – with passive listening you are just physically in the range of the audio. When you actively listen you choose to hear the words that are being said and everything in between.

Be 'present' and get the environment right – if you want to really listen then cut out distractions. Both the physical ones like other noise, an uncomfortable chair or people interrupting you, and also mental distractions, such as what you need to do when you get home from work.

Avoid formulating an answer too soon – often we do not listen so well as we are developing what we are going to say next in our heads. Try to focus clearly on what is being said.

Show that you are listening – lean slightly towards the person speaking, verbally or physically acknowledge that you are hearing what they are saying and use this opportunity to build trust and encourage openness.

Avoid interrupting or judging – however keen you are to share your thoughts. Hold on until the other person has finished speaking. Do not interrupt them unless it is an emergency. Also try to put any bias you may have aside. This could have been built up as part of your culture or a past experience. Either way it may not be relevant so you should listen with an open mind.

Ask the right questions – you can choose questions that will draw out more information or clarify points to help you to understand what someone is saying better than if they just told you. These questions could be:

- What I am hearing is … Is that correct?

- Help me to understand this better. Can you give me an example?

- I really want to understand you. Can you explain how this all started?

- What could we do differently to avoid it happening again?

- How can I help you? What would make a difference for you?

Ideas to make your communication even more effective

Only 7 per cent of communication received is the actual content that is communicated, so how can you use your **tone, body language and the environment**, in which the communication is delivered, to achieve a better understanding? Every interaction, when you have teachers or parents or students in the room (or even when you communicate online), is a valuable **opportunity to learn**. It shouldn't just be about what you can 'tell' them.

Consider **sending information to people before your meeting** so the valuable face-to-face time can be spent on discussion, building understanding and interaction. You can do this with teachers, students or parents. If you share information in advance with teachers then they will come with questions. If you do so with parents then you won't need to spend time explaining your message and you can have a useful discussion instead. Doing so with students is a way to flip learning on its head and give them the material early and then use the lesson time to answer questions and queries so they go away even more informed.

Try to **anticipate any areas of confusion** and concern and how you will deal with them. Maybe even draft out a page of potential questions that you can share with other school leaders so you are all repeating similar messages. Think about how the receivers may have **different preferences for how they receive information**. For example, some people relate better if they have visual images and others when they have lots of facts and figures.

Managing more challenging communication

Some situations require more sensitivity in communicating. Dealing with aggressive reactions, delivering bad news, and engaging with uninterested parents are three examples of this.

Dealing with aggressive reactions

Sometimes you may experience people who react aggressively when you communicate with them. This could include shouting, swearing, personal insults, verbal threats, threatening gestures, sarcasm or harassment. However, reactions could be subtler when people become passionate about a particular subject and start to raise their voice. You can do a number of things to manage aggressive reactions and avoid them escalating into something bigger.

Stay calm and composed. Speak in a calm voice and keep your body language assertive but not aggressive (maintain eye contact, stand or sit tall, don't fold your arms across your chest or fidget), even if you are feeling uncomfortable.

Keep yourself safe. Ensure that you have some space between you and the person who is being aggressive and know how you might move out of the situation if you need to.

Acknowledge that you've heard them. If someone is expressing their opinion in an aggressive way, let them have their say until they have made their point. Acknowledge that you have heard the person's view.

Take it offline. If you are in a larger group and the issue is specific to this person, then it would be better to discuss it with them individually. Reassure them that to understand the issue fully and help them you would like to discuss it after the event.

Ask the right questions. Ask questions to understand if they know the implications of how they are reacting to put the focus back on them.

Be prepared. If it is a matter that concerns others, then it's important to go into events as prepared as possible so you can be ready for challenging reactions. Do some research amongst staff and find out what they think people might ask about. You can even ask some friendly parents to give their views. This way you can be fully prepared to give a factual and helpful response that will close down any concerns.

Know the boundaries. If the person gets beyond a point where you are comfortable then you need to express that their behaviour is not acceptable on school grounds or towards you. Ask them to discuss the point again when they have calmed down. You can, if you have a parent partnership agreement in place and they are a parent, refer to this and explain that both of you need to put the interests of the student first and that this behaviour isn't helping. Explain the consequences if they continue in the same aggressive manner.

Don't take it personally. If it starts to get personal, then you need to avoid reacting and steer them back to the facts. Let them know that it feels personal and that is not going to help anyone. Ask questions to get to the root of the problem so you can keep your responses objective and potentially find a way forward.

Delivering bad news

Sadly, you can't deliver good news every day. So what is the best way to deliver bad news? Firstly, it depends on who the bad news impacts. For example, if it is of a personal nature such as someone is being made redundant or being sacked then clearly you'll do this on a one-to-one basis with the right evidence or reasoning to justify your decision. But what about where you need to deliver bad news that has a more wide sweeping impact, on teachers, students and parents?

An example could be a cut in funding leading to a reduction in extra-curricular classes or that planning permission has not been granted for a new education facility that is desperately needed. You can take the following steps to support the best outcome.

Develop a communication mindset. Go through the steps above.

Build a cast iron Q&A. Be prepared for potential questions by putting yourself in the shoes of the different audiences and imagine what they may be thinking and feeling.

Ensure your leadership team can support you. Brief your leadership team and Board of Governors before you need to communicate. Ensure they can speak on behalf of the school. You are a team and should speak with one voice.

Communicate in a timely way. Don't wait too long or you'll find the news gets out in the wrong way and rumours cannot be contained. Be proactive and communicate as quickly as possible. Follow up this communication regularly if appropriate.

Show you care and empathise. When you communicate show how disappointed you are too. Be as open as possible with the facts.

Come up with other options. Can you or your team provide alternative ideas that may need support from the community? For example, could you make an arrangement with another local school to use their facility?

Give people space to ask questions. You may feel nervous about inviting too many questions but it is best to get them out in the open. You should be well prepared with Q&As and if you don't have answers just say so, obviously aiming to find one wherever possible.

Be ready to speak to the media. After you have communicated with relevant school audiences verbally and in writing then, if the story potentially has media interest, reach out to local newspapers and radio stations to be proactive in your message. Or at least have a reactive statement with agreed wording in case you are approached. See Chapter 13 about crisis communication for bigger news that you may need to handle.

Engaging uninterested parents

Students achieve more when schools work in partnership with parents. But some parents may have had a bad experience of school themselves or may not be interested in their child's education.

So what can you do to engage this hard to reach group? You could invite parents to 'free' classes that build their skills in life but also have a knock on effect of supporting their children. One example may be where you have parents whose first language is not English, and they could struggle to understand some of your communication. You could offer short English language sessions on the school grounds to get them over the threshold. This will start to change their perception of 'school' and breaks down barriers so they feel more positive about supporting their child's education. The investment in time will be worth the outcome.

There is a lot to take in from this chapter. We did say at the start of it that communication impacts around 80 per cent of what you do so it's only natural there will be a lot to learn. Try to learn one step at a time by focusing on different aspects that we have covered in this chapter. You could, for example, start by improving your listening skills. Once you have mastered listening, put that into practice when dealing with challenging parents. It will take time to build your skills but you and your school will benefit from you doing so. In the next chapter we will look at how to take your communication skills to the next level to really inspire and motivate your audiences.

Top three take-aways:

1 We all need to improve how we communicate, however good we think we are.

2 Plan and prepare for your communication wherever possible.

3 Look for ways to further improve how you communicate through being self-aware and really understanding your audience.

9 Inspire and motivate

In the previous chapter, we shared some ideas to help you build your communication skills. In this chapter we look at how you and your leadership team can take these skills to the next level so you inspire and motivate those around you. You clearly set the standards, culture and direction for everyone else in your school, so being able to inspire and motivate is critical if you want to stand out from the crowd.

According to the National Standards, you (as a school leader) need to be able to communicate compellingly the school's vision and drive strategic leadership, empowering all pupils and staff to excel. During an Ofsted or ISI inspection, you are measured on how well the vision and ambition for your school is communicated to staff, parents and pupils.

Every day, every time

Leadership isn't something you do just in formal situations. You need to develop your leadership communication skills so they become effortless (they become part of your being) and apply them in every interaction with parents, teachers and students – even when you think no one is looking. If you demonstrate great leadership communication, inspire and act with integrity, then you can build trust, bringing both teachers and parents behind your vision to achieve better student outcomes and results for your school.

Sadly, despite building trust, it takes just one wrong move to damage relationships. This doesn't just reflect on you personally but also obviously impacts the reputation of your school.

> *"It takes many good deeds to build a good reputation, and only one bad one to lose it."*
> Benjamin Franklin

So what makes someone an inspirational communicator? Inspirational communicators use style, tone of voice, body movements and engagement of everyone in the room to create a sense that they are connecting fully with their audience. They motivate and inspire people to be better. They deliver success through other people. Take a look at some of your favourite speakers on YouTube, observing what makes them good, then think about which attributes they have that you can comfortably apply yourself. It's important that you don't look like you are 'acting' but you are your true, authentic self.

If we look more broadly at leadership communication, we know that this is an area where a lot of leaders struggle. The 2014 Ketchum Leadership Communication Monitor reported:

> *Open communication remains critical to effective leadership – again the top-ranking attribute, with 74 per cent viewing it as very important to great leadership – yet only 29 per cent feel leaders communicate effectively with a 45-point expectation/delivery gap.*

Education leadership is clearly no different. So, if you find being an inspirational communicator challenging, then you're not alone. Fortunately, you can take steps to improve. Here is our ten-point framework for inspirational communication.

1   Understand who the leaders are who need to inspire

2   Assess how inspiring you are right now

3   Create your inspirational 'North Star'

4   Build your team

5   It's the little things that count

6   Support your team in learning from each other

7   Watch your language

8   The power of stories

9   Get emotional

10 Planning your inspirational communication

Understand who the leaders are who need to inspire

There are many ways to look at leadership. It may not just apply to those at the top in the traditional hierarchy. Generally, in this section, we refer to *leadership* as being the headteacher and their leadership team. However, the Board of Governors needs to share the same common purpose, and work together talking with one voice, maintaining the same high standards of inspirational and motivational communication.

Assess how inspiring you are right now

There are a number of things leaders can do to understand how inspirational and motivational their communication is right now. Take the test at the start of this book (see Chapter 3). Film one of your presentations, watching it back with a critical eye. Or simply ask people for honest feedback after you communicate.

Whichever way you find out how you are doing, it shouldn't be a one-off review. Regularly ask your team members for suggestions on how they think you could collectively be more inspiring based on what they are all hearing and seeing. Ask them what you can do personally to better support them, listening to questions and concerns. Be clear at the end of every meeting about exactly what you are communicating as a result – who needs to know, who is responsible for discussing/ sharing and what do you need back from the audience to measure their feedback, their action or understanding. Ensure that you follow up any feedback with a response or action, and tell people you've taken action to encourage even more open feedback.

Create your inspirational 'North Star'

Everyone needs to know what is expected of them – how they fit into your school and, importantly, not just what the school does, but why it does it. This needs to be articulated through your school's vision. As outlined earlier in the book, you should define your vision statement together with your leadership team. It should have the input of teachers and parents. Your vision and values become the guiding star for all you do. Everyone at your school should be able to talk about them in a way that inspires people and has meaning for all. And most importantly, the leadership team needs to live them every day.

Every individual in your school wants to know what their job is, how this fits into where the school is going, how they are doing in their job and, of course, whether leaders and colleagues care about them. So when you communicate your vision, you need to tap into these themes and support your leadership team in creating a view of what this means to every person in the team. In other words, what does it mean to me? This can be done very simply through the following steps.

Spend time, as a leadership team, thinking about what excites you about the vision. Understand where you collectively see barriers and have concerns. Work together to identify ways to overcome these barriers and concerns. Importantly think about examples of where you are already doing things that prove you are delivering on your vision. Put yourselves in the shoes of your teachers: what will excite them and what will they see as barriers? You can now develop examples and stories of where you are delivering successfully to address the barriers and emphasise those things that will excite everyone. You will have the stories to engage people in your vision but in ways that have meaning and connect emotionally.

You can apply this approach to other audiences, whether they are parents or students or the Board of Governors.

Build your team

There are number of things that you can do to build your team through better communication. These can help to speed up and improve how you work together, reduce misunderstandings, create stronger relationships and ensure you speak with one voice.

Know your **own leadership style,** and realise that how you communicate impacts your team. Keep learning and improving where you know you have areas for improvement.

Have **regular meetings** with a pre-agreed agenda to create a good structure for your communication. Rotate who takes notes and actions, and refer back to these at the next meeting. Always have a point on the agenda to be clear on what you should all be communicating from the meeting and any items that should not be shared at this stage.

Know one another by understanding the people beyond their names and positions. Consider a social event or team-building event where you can really get to understand each other better and build relationships.

Recognise your different backgrounds and skills and how **different knowledge and perspectives** brings richness and makes you a team. Also identify where you have gaps that maybe need to be filled in other ways.

Invest in some **regular communication coaching** as a team. Better understand each other's **communication styles** (beyond just introvert/extrovert) so you can look beyond immediate reactions. Use this to understand the good intentions and how this may be being expressed differently from how you would do it. Remember that just because it is different doesn't mean it is wrong!

It's the little things that count

You may have heard this said before but it is really true. A simple 'thank you' can make all the difference after a long, hard day. Or maybe a quick email or, better still, a written note. Human beings generally want to feel valued. Often when times are tough and leaders get busy, then the important 'little things' are forgotten. People can become stressed and neglect the things that matter, like their health and well-being. This leads to increased sickness rates and 'presenteeism', i.e. they turn up to work but they're not there mentally.

Spend the little time it takes to say thank you. Encourage others to do it throughout your school and make sure it isn't just reserved for the 'big stuff'. Recognise the small things too. Support well-being through role-modelling healthy living, wherever possible, showing that you're balancing your work and life well. It's not just about the number of steps you take a day but how healthy you are mentally and physically. Consider seeking external support to come and talk to your team about mental health and well-being. If you have a school medical centre, then empower them to take the lead and create a group focused on school well-being, not just for the students. This will support you in building energy, motivation and creating advocates among your team.

Support your team in learning from each other

Teachers have great ideas about how to improve your school. If they are all taking action separately then you won't feel the benefit. There will be duplication when teachers are already under time pressures.

Create opportunities to bring staff together to discuss important issues and work out solutions together. Show them that you value their opinions and recognise when people come up with proactive ideas. Ensure you create an environment where mistakes are turned into learning, rather than something that is buried and best forgotten. Consider informal brainstorming sessions to open up creative thinking and let people know that you welcome their views. Take action so the ideas are used and recognise where the ideas came from. Ensure your team stays in touch with what's happening in the outside world, the latest trends and thinking. Encourage people to share what they are hearing with the team to focus on forward thinking.

Watch your language

"Words can inspire. Words can destroy. Choose yours well."

Robin Sharma

The language you use and how you enable people to do their work make a difference. For example, you could say that you want someone to build a solution that you have in mind. But if you are surrounded by experts, why not share the issue you are facing and ask them for the best way to solve it? You should try to benefit from their different perspectives rather than just giving them the solution. You are also then telling them that you value their expertise, and you'll achieve a better result together.

The power of stories

Storytelling can be powerful. Through developing your own stories, you can bring to life things that could actually be quite boring. Human beings (and our brains) love stories; in fact, according to Jerome Bruner, a cognitive psychologist, we are 22 times more likely to remember something when it is told as a story. Stories have a start, a middle and an end. They have key characters and they are part of your culture. Draw them from your personal experience and relate them to your topic to build meaningful communication. See the guidance in Appendix 9.1 to help you develop your story.

Getting emotional

Showing feelings and emotion isn't something that comes naturally in many organisations, and certainly not to some leaders. However, there are real benefits in building 'emotional intelligence'. And if this doesn't come naturally to you, make sure you have people in your leadership team who do have high levels of emotional intelligence so they can support you. There are five components of emotional intelligence (according to Daniel Goleman, an American psychologist):

Self-awareness – those who know that how they feel and what they do and say impacts other people.

Self-regulation – those people who stay in control and don't attack others or rush decisions.

Motivation – self-motivated people who maintain high standards of delivery.

Empathy – those who have the ability to put themselves in someone else's shoes.

Social skills – these people have great communication skills, are good listeners with the ability to inspire, motivate and praise their teams.

Planning your inspirational communication

Similar to how you planned your communication in the previous chapter, think about how you would prepare for a major parent or teacher meeting. You will likely have a list of things you want to cover. You may have spent some time focusing on this content, perhaps even rehearsed in front of the mirror a few times. But you can achieve a better result by trying the following simple approach. (See Appendix 9.2 for a template to guide your preparation.)

1 **Determine your ultimate outcome:** What is the ultimate outcome of what you want to say? What is the journey you want to take people on? Can you share any of your experiences and tell a story that brings this to life? Use the answers to these questions as the foundation for your message.

2 **Create the environment for great communication:** Reflect on the mood of the people in your audience. Have they just rushed there from a busy day of lessons? Is it just before lunch? Are they busy parents who have rushed in from work? Beginning with an initial comment that recognises and shows appreciation for your audience's current situation will immediately put people at ease and demonstrate your empathy.

3 **The big opening:** Don't let this be daunting – you don't need to be the world's greatest orator to find a way to immediately grab people's attention. Your opening could be a slightly provocative question or a surprising fact or statistic.

4 **The take-aways:** It is important to be clear about what you want people to take away. If someone asked them after the event what you said, then what would they remember? List a maximum of three short themes as a constant focus of your presentation. How can you make those relevant for this audience? What do you want them to know, feel and do as a result?

5 **Make it a conversation:** You can make what you say a conversation, even with 100 people in front of you. Find ways to ask questions. For example, ask for a show of hands around a topic to understand your audience and bring them on board. Ask for willing volunteers to share their views to bring what you are saying to life. It will help to keep people's interest. Remember, people will lose interest quickly if you just talk *at* them.

6 **How you present yourself:** The words we say make up 7 per cent of our communication. Whether you are communicating face to face, on video or by phone, the tone of voice and body language elements become very powerful in conveying feelings or attitudes. But all sorts of things can take over and disrupt the flow when we share a message in different environments. These could include nerves, the environment itself, or a difficult question that interrupts our train of thought. Generally, most of us don't really know how others perceive us in these situations. This is why rehearsal is key.

   Take at least twice as much time to rehearse as you might think to deliver important messages. Prepare for meetings and think about how you can say things in different ways to achieve a better outcome. Remember to exhale before you begin to speak.

   Manage the speed at which you share an idea. This is called your 'rate of ideas'. Most of us, when on the receiving end, can take on a new idea, but we get confused if we get thrown lots of information all at once. So, once you have shared an idea, pause slightly to allow people to take that in. Enunciate and speak clearly, especially if you have an international audience.

   Voice coaching can be effective to help with better voice projection, clarity and rate of ideas.

   How you present yourself will also communicate a lot about you. You need to dress appropriately for the occasion, venue and audience.

7 **Close and repeat:** Bring what you are saying to a logical close, and say what you just said – succinctly remind people of your key message(s). Remind them of any specific actions you want them to take, and then thank them for their time.

8 **How did you do?** Ask some people what they took from the event and how you could improve for next time. Demonstrate that you are always learning, which

shows you want others to continue to improve as well. If you have the opportunity, ask someone to video-record you at an event and play it back. It may be painful watching yourself, but you can learn so much that way.

The above steps are also useful (to a lesser degree) for informal interactions. Keep this approach in mind, put it into practice and see the difference it makes.

Adjust your style to your audience

Not all audiences are alike! Much like with people of different learning types, people prefer to communicate in different ways. Some prefer to hear things, some to see and some to experience. There are those who can immediately digest information and think on their feet, saying their thoughts for all to hear. There are others who prefer to take in the information, evaluate it and form thoughtful responses. They may not want to speak out in front of others in the same way. So how do you lead teams with all these different preferences and still be a great communicator?

The answer is to be flexible in your style and approach. For example, when you are asking people to consider new information, send out some key points before the meeting and give people time to digest these with clear guidelines as to what you would like to achieve in the meeting. This will enable those who like 'thinking time' to prepare. It will also mean better use of your time in meetings; the focus can be on the discussion and interaction rather than information sharing.

When you are presenting to larger groups, you need to connect with everyone whatever their communication preference. Use storytelling to create a 'picture' in those visual-people's minds. Include practical experience, for those who are kinaesthetic, which brings your message to life. Include brainstorming and questions and answers for those whose preference is auditory.

The way you and your senior school leaders behave and communicate will set the standard for your school. In this chapter we have provided you with a framework to ensure your communication is inspirational and engaging in the long term. The most important factor to remember is you have to be clear on what you want to happen as a result, and shape how you communicate accordingly. We will leave the topic of personal communication now, and move to, in the next five chapters, explaining how to avoid some of the many pitfalls of communication.

Top three take-aways:

1 How well leaders communicate can make or break your school's reputation.

2 Invest time in getting it right at every interaction and every day.

3 Prepare for communication opportunities and maximize them.

Case study: The inspirational headteacher

In the example of Strawberry Mansion High School in North Philadelphia, Linda Cliatt-Wayman (Principal) shows the difference inspirational communication can make. She has made great progress in turning around a low-performing and persistently dangerous school through her determination to lead — and to love the students, no matter what. Linda has shown how the little things really matter, through the respect she has achieved, by doing simple things like managing the lunchroom every day. She speaks with the students, asks them questions, and even though she can't sing at all, she sings each one happy birthday. She has monthly town hall meetings, so students can ask real questions and she gives real answers. Linda believes in an exchange in love and listening. She also empowers and asks her staff for their collective views to improve the school, taking her team with her at every step.

Importantly she is clear about her expectations and her vision, and reminds them every day that education can change their lives.

10 Stop the overload

Information is power. Information is also everywhere, but time is scarce. Everyone, including parents and teachers, is now bombarded with more and more information every day, and only a limited amount of time to digest it and prioritise what is important. The reality is that information overload causes problems that negatively affect children's education. As a result of 'lost' or unread important communication, children turn up without the right equipment, without money for trips and miss deadlines. Parents may miss important meetings, causing teachers to become stressed. Earlier in the book we looked at prioritising your audiences for communication. In this chapter, we discuss how to avoid overloading your audiences with too much information.

Reduce the overload on teachers

From our research with parents, we know that they want to contact teachers directly. When we asked parents how their school could improve communication with them, one thing they suggested was to make better use of email messaging. Some schools have provided email addresses for all teachers. Others are concerned that teachers are pressured enough without having an additional mailbox to manage. Our advice is that if you decide to open up email addresses for all teachers, then manage the expectations of parents.

Firstly, parents should only email directly when it is important and there are no other means to communicate. Provide etiquette guidelines (and preferably training) for your teaching staff so they know how to respond appropriately and reduce the pressure on them.

Asking parents for feedback is often seen as opening the floodgates. However, they will still want to share their views even if you decide to keep them closed. Parents will just have critical conversations where you can't hear them, but where they could be even more damaging to your reputation.

Give parents the opportunity to discuss their views through well managed 'quick polls' on your website, email surveys or parent discussion forums around specific topics. By giving them these outlets, you'll reduce the ad hoc requests to teachers. If you are receiving the same question over and over again, then create a Frequently Asked Questions section for parents on your website and direct them there.

Take a planned approach to information management

You want parents to read and understand the information that is most important to them so they can work in partnership with your school to achieve the best outcomes for their children. Through taking some simple steps, you can ensure good information management that makes this happen.

Having children and parents in the right place at the right time is a good starting point, but ideally you want to ensure that your really important messages get through. Aim for getting the right information to parents, with the appropriate amount of priority attached, to enable them to make timely and informed decisions about their children.

Here are eight steps you can take to avoid information overload in your school:

1 Choose an approach that aligns to your vision and sets you apart

2 Remember your audiences

3 Prioritise your messages

4 Make the most of face-to-face opportunities

5 Practice 'air traffic control'

6 Use a 'traffic light' system

7 Find an owner

8 Be clear on the parent's role in the partnership

Choose an approach that aligns to your vision and sets you apart

Your approach to information management (processes and systems) should reflect your vision. For example, if your focus is to create independence for students then you should think about how your communication practices reflect this. If it's about creating accountability, then make the appropriate people accountable in the communication processes. And if it's about being a high achiever, ensure that your communication is high quality and highly organised, and delivered in a robust and managed manner.

Remember your audiences

To enable information to be targeted at the right people, break down your audience groups into those people who you communicate with often. Create lists that can be managed and kept up-to-date by an appropriate member of staff. You also need to agree who should coordinate communication with each audience.

The audience lists may include the Board of Governors, school leadership team, all teachers, all school staff, parents by year group or parents by class. It can get tricky when you have parents with more than one child in the same school in different years who don't want to receive unnecessary or duplicate information. In this case it's important to reduce duplication wherever possible when setting up these lists.

Prioritise your messages

Decide how you will communicate with these various audience groups. This should also be driven by what needs to be communicated. For example, when you have an urgent message for parents, you want to get it to them directly with the minimal chance of delay, so a direct text message or email is probably best. Use a 'return receipt' to understand how many people have actually opened the email. However, if you use email for every communication, parents will start ignoring those they think are less urgent and subsequently miss those that are urgent. Make sure your emails are titled with a clear message, such as 'for action' or 'for information', to make the difference in urgency clear.

Make the most of face-to-face opportunities

There are a number of times during the year that parents come into the school, such as new parents' meetings, parents' evenings, school plays or events. This is precious time when you have the attention of the parents. Use this valuable time to share your school's important messages, but, importantly, use this time to gather their input and suggestions and encourage them to help each other to find solutions to the challenges their children are facing. Avoid using the time to just pass on information that could have been shared in other ways.

Practice 'air traffic control'

Once you have identified your audience groups, established who is responsible for communicating with them and decided on which communication channels to use, it's time to create your 'air traffic control' system. Just like a real air traffic control tower, this system designates clear roles and responsibilities so that everyone knows which voice to listen to and clashes (or crashes) are avoided and everything 'lands' safely. This is a process that follows the steps outlined previously, but mapped to a calendar. Wherever possible, ensure that regular daily, weekly or monthly communication is scheduled and visible to everyone. Once they are, it is easier to see the impact of adding something else to the list.

Use a 'traffic light' system

A great way to clearly prioritise communication is to introduce a 'traffic light' system (see Figure 10.1). Red means urgent or 'must read', amber means the information is 'important but not for immediate action' and green means 'nice to know', for information only. Ensure all teachers know the traffic-light approach. You'll reduce the number of questions from parents, increase the number of parents who actually do what they need to do within your timescales and create clarity for teachers. See the example in Figure 10.1 of what this could look like.

Find an owner

This whole process usually requires at least one responsible owner to ensure great information management. This is someone who will challenge others if communication happens that isn't planned and will ensure the schedule is kept up to date. You may need some external help to enable you to stand back and take stock, putting the framework and training in place and then you can entrust the process to a couple of staff members to ensure this happens seamlessly and every time. Consistency builds trust.

Be clear on the parent's role in the partnership

Parents have told us they want more information, they don't know where to go to find out what already exists, but they also receive too much information from their school. It is clear there are some misaligned expectations from parents about their school communication and their role in the process.

When new students join your school, set out your expectations of their parents as part of the partnership and communication process. Tell the parents what you will provide to them and when, where to go for more information and to ask questions. Make it clear what you need from them, e.g. participation at parent meetings or feedback on communication. Provide this in writing and ask them to sign an agreement of the 'partnership' you are both embarking on, to help their child to become the best they can be. See an example of a guide to school information in Appendix 10.1.

Too much information is often worse than none at all. Having a better idea of this common pitfall of many school communication systems and how to avoid it will make everyone's lives easier. In the next chapter, we look at how you can use technology to help you manage communication with your audiences.

Red:
- Used for urgent and important information.
- Top three points should be sent by text also.
- Always requires school leadership sign off.
- Examples, closure of school or child safety issue.

Amber:
- Used for important but not urgent information.
- Top three points should be sent by email also.
- Examples, change to term dates or school trip that requires parent consent.

Green:
- Used for 'nice to know' information.
- Top three points should be available on the website or similar.
- Examples, school family day or school uniform sale.

Standard Template for each traffic light colour

Urgent: [add subject]

Top three points
Make it clear what is for action or information with a deadline.
1.
2.
3.

Further information:
Add additional places people can find further information.

Contact for questions:

Important: [add subject]

Top three points
Make it clear what is for action or information with a deadline.
1.
2.
3.

Further information:
Add additional places people can find further information.

Contact for questions:

For information: [add subject]

Top three points
Include the what, why, how, where and when?
1.
2.
3.

Further information:
Add additional places people can find further information.

Contact for questions:

Figure 10.1 A simple traffic-light approach to managing school information

Top three take-aways:

1 Less information is often better.

2 Different communication requires different methods.

3 You need parents to be able to quickly identify crucial messages.

Take the technology advantage

Our world is becoming ever more technological, and the expectations of students, parents and teachers are high when it comes to communicating using technology. People want to communicate with their school in the same way they do in their daily lives, using smart phones, apps and social media. They expect to be able to make payments and complete forms online. They want personalised information that meets their needs and is easily searchable. In the previous chapter, we discussed information overload. Technology is an area that can easily result in even more information overload if it isn't managed properly. This chapter aims to help you to identify ways to use technology to your advantage.

Time for the twenty-first century

Difficult to navigate and out of date websites, paper forms and money in envelopes would not position your school well. These would create frustration and a perception your school is stuck in the past or slow to adopt new technology. Importantly the right technology can save your school time and money. It is essential though, as stated earlier in this book, to be led by the vision of your school rather than being led by technology. Technology can provide some solutions, but there are lots of options. Schools, like many organisations, struggle with technology for a number of reasons.

Technology is just a tool

As mentioned in the previous chapter, there are so many sources of potential information going out from a school. Information goes to parents (and teachers) from different places, in different formats, often with no clear designation of what is a priority and what is a 'nice to have'. These differing sources create confusion and overload recipients, especially if parents have more than one child at school and receive everything in duplicate. Technology can help to reduce this overload but only if used well. You need school staff who are trained, and a clear information strategy. This will ensure the right information reaches the right people in the right way to achieve your outcome.

Technology needs people

Even if you have a clear approach to information management and the best technology, you still need one person who really coordinates this in the school and ensures everyone sticks to those standards.

Technology may not be the issue

A valuable first step is to listen to parents, teachers and students, so that you get to the root cause of issues before throwing money at various technology upgrades or overhauls. For example, a school may decide to invest in a new website, but this is not the communication issue facing parents who are overloaded with information and can't find what they need when they need it. A new website would potentially make this problem worse for parents.

Technology needs to be two-way

Using the right tools to get information to parents at the right time is crucial. Many of these tools can also be used to collect feedback and insights from parents. Two-way communication through technology should be an ongoing and simple process rather than a once-a-year parent survey that takes 20 minutes to complete and weeks to analyse and action.

Technology and information management go hand in hand

Schools may have one or the other – a good technology system that is poorly used or good processes that require manual intervention. Having the right technology together with the right information management system is a winning formula for parents and school personnel alike.

Your options

Through our research we know that parents want information that is relevant to them, that is clearly prioritised and available through the same tools they use on a daily basis. They want mobile-friendly communication, with information online that they can immediately see and determine what is important and urgent. They need to know where to find additional information and be able to access it easily. The best technology options integrate a number of areas into one system.

Your face to the world

This is likely to be your website, or mobile app if you have one. Anyone interested in learning more about your school will expect you to have a website as a minimum requirement. Your website should feature videos, audio and photos, as well as text. Importantly, build it to reflect your school vision, based on your audiences' needs – not just what you want to tell people. Use it to make you stand out from the crowd.

Building a parent community

You may use a number of different online tools to help you manage school life, such as an online payment system, a homework platform or a school shop, in addition to other essentials including the school calendar, attendance records and online forms. Your website is the starting point for parents to access these tools, which provides you with a fantastic opportunity to build a parent community. Use your website to share engaging content such as video diaries with children speaking about events, images of artwork and sports successes. Provide parents with a forum where they can share their views on key topics, with polls and surveys to gather snapshot data. This is much better than having them discuss it on Facebook or another online social media website.

Building your school team

It is equally important to ensure your school team has a common place that will help to build a school community. You cannot rely on emails alone. Ideally using the same or a similar platform to the one hosting your website, you need to provide your school community with a common place to share resources, ideas and the latest in education thinking; to ask questions of colleagues; and to have online discussions. This type of private network, more commonly known as an 'intranet', is a great way to build your school community and encourage sharing across different areas of your school.

Fast access to important and urgent information

Parents need important and urgent information pushed to them, rather than expecting them to go and search for it. The best way to do this is by sending a message to their registered mobile device(s) by using a bulk SMS system. This is often more immediate than email and usually allows you to monitor when messages have been received and read. While this may not seem like a key requirement, having the ability to contact every parent at your school quickly in the event of an emergency is a critical way to keep their children safe and your reputation intact.

Students experience a 'modern school environment' and are engaged

Children use technology at home from an early age so it is natural for them to expect technology to be an integral part of the classroom and their learning journey. Encouraging them to participate in discussion forums, post blogs and produce videos will develop their communication skills in an engaging way. Technology can also enable 'flipped learning' where typical lecture and homework elements of a course are reversed, meaning short video lectures are viewed by students at home before the class session, so time in class is devoted to more informed and more engaging discussions. The use of cloud-based systems to communicate in class also provides an opportunity to better involve parents in real time so that issues can be identified and addressed quickly.

Which technology should I use?

This really depends on your vision, what you want to achieve, the resources you have available and the needs of your audiences. As we have already suggested, a website is a prerequisite for any school today, as it is for almost any business. However, just because you have a nice looking website doesn't mean it is good for the parents. It needs to convey what your school is about, be engaging, and it needs to be easy to find critical information. Then you should make use of some of the many tools that facilitate parent tasks such as making online payments and integrate these into your website.

Developing an online place for your team to collaborate is, in our view, critical to school harmony and the development of your school community. SMS messaging technology is also crucial, and it is very accessible, with many platforms to choose from depending on your requirements.

Once you have the basics in place, you can move on to more advanced communication options such as using cloud-based technology to enable flipped learning and better parental involvement. You should remember though, technology in itself is not communication. You need meaningful content that helps to convey your key messages and supports your school vision.

In the next chapter, we look at how technology tools and managing information overload, as discussed in the previous chapters, helps you to manage change within your school.

Top three take-aways:

1 Technology is an enabler of communication for any school.

2 Decide which platform(s) to use based on the needs of your audience.

3 A great piece of technology is no substitute for good content.

12 Communicating change

Most human beings don't like change. It's the way we are wired. So when a school makes a major change, like joins a multi-academy trust, appoints a new head-teacher, or even when there are external government-led changes to education, the school needs to invest in some planned communication. This will ensure they take people successfully through the change with them.

It is important to spend time communicating about change before it happens. Failure to do so will almost certainly result in a fall in motivation and decline in productivity, fuelled by people talking about the change negatively – both inside and outside of school. Some teachers may even become ill or leave due to stress. This could all damage the school's reputation.

In this chapter we explain the stages that people go through when they experience change. They may not go through all of these stages in exactly this sequence, but the aim is to keep people out of the 'deep dip', able to make it to 'the other side' feeling positive and able to move forward (see Figure 12.1).

Let's use an example that would affect you directly: a new headteacher joining a school. This type of change can potentially create a period of instability and concern at the school if the new headteacher is unknown to the rest of the teaching staff and parents. There might be a real sense of loss if the previous headteacher was respected and liked. Here are ten steps a school can take to successfully support a change of this nature. If you are the incoming or outgoing headteacher, use this as a checkpoint for success.

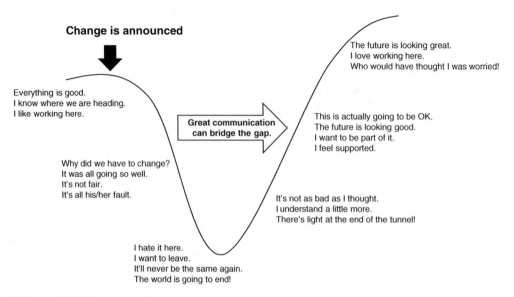

Change is announced

Everything is good.
I know where we are heading.
I like working here.

The future is looking great.
I love working here.
Who would have thought I was worried!

Great communication can bridge the gap.

This is actually going to be OK.
The future is looking good.
I want to be part of it.
I feel supported.

Why did we have to change?
It was all going so well.
It's not fair.
It's all his/her fault.

It's not as bad as I thought.
I understand a little more.
There's light at the end of the tunnel!

I hate it here.
I want to leave.
It'll never be the same again.
The world is going to end!

Figure 12.1   The change curve

Communicate as early as possible

In our example, you should work with the Board of Governors, and if possible, the outgoing and incoming headteachers, to plan how and when you will communicate with each of your school audiences. It is critical that this is done in the right order to achieve the right outcome.

Some considerations when communicating a change like this will include trying to tell people face to face wherever possible. If you can't do it face to face, then at least speak to people by phone rather than have them hear it from a colleague or read it in an email. You should tell the leadership team first, then teachers, then parents and students. You also need to be prepared to proactively tell the media (and in fact announce on social media and your website) at the same time as you tell parents to ensure you successfully manage the message externally.

Have your story and facts clear

Involve your new headteacher as early as possible. A key reason for this is so that you can work with him or her and the Board of Governors to agree on your story. Aligning the appointment to your school values and vision and having the new headteacher make reference to them will give comfort to existing parents and students. Put yourself in the shoes of teachers, parents, students and the local community. What will they want to know about the appointment? How will you answer their questions? To help you and others who might be asked the same questions, you should create a thorough question and answer document and make it available to those who are likely to be asked.

Find the silver lining

Emphasise why the new headteacher will be good for the school, talk about their relevant experience, but particularly talk about their passion for coming to work at the school. As previously mentioned, you should try to demonstrate how they will support your school's vision, to avoid creating a perception that everything will change when they arrive. You should include a photo of the new headteacher with any written communication, as this makes the communication more personal.

If it's possible, arrange a series of short video clips from the new headteacher to create a really good first impression. Use these to show to current and prospective parents, teachers and students as an introduction of sorts, prior to the new headteacher being able to come and meet them in person. Personal videos give a greater sense of the headteacher as a person, rather than faceless text-based communication.

Share evidence about how it will be better

If possible, arrange for parents or students from the headteacher's previous school to provide some short quotes about the strengths of the new headteacher and the positive impact he or she had on that school. Also, share any accolades or positive media coverage from his or her past school. Such evidence will help 'sell' the person who will lead the school, and give your school's community faith in the decision made.

Be open, honest and consistent

This point is particularly critical to get things off on the right footing. Be clear about why the current headteacher is leaving and what is happening and when. If there are reasons that limit what you can say, then be open about this rather than try to hide it. This tactic will prevent the media from seeking out or creating a story that could ultimately damage your school's reputation, even if the story is incorrect.

Keep the message consistent no matter who is speaking. Take care that the leadership team has talking points and prepared answers to common questions so you can talk as a unified team. If leaders don't know the answer to the question, then they should say they don't know, but will get back to the person with an answer quickly. It is also important that you discuss the feedback you are receiving as a leadership team and agree if you need to make changes to how you are communicating as a result.

Be patient, visible and listen to people's views

A fact of modern life is that life goes on; today's headlines are tomorrow's history. Nevertheless, senior leaders of your school need to take the time to get out of their offices and talk to parents, other teachers and students on a regular basis. Even if you find this frustrating, be patient. The time you invest in listening, and responding, will be appreciated.

Make regular listening a priority and empathise

Keep listening at all times, not just for a day or two after an announcement is made. You could, for example, have drop-in coffee sessions for parents, or implement an open door policy at certain times of the day for school staff or students. You should also rotate the 'listening' amongst your leadership team so it doesn't just sit with the headteacher. In doing so, you should ensure your leadership team is able to demonstrate a level of empathy and find ways to move people forward positively.

Remove the concerns that you've heard

Agree on a way to capture all the questions the leadership team is receiving where you might not have agreed answers. We have provided a template to help you with this (Appendix 12.1). You should work with the new headteacher to build answers to these questions and keep posting them on your website so people know there is one place to go for updates. Make sure that the leadership team is referring to these answers when talking to people to allay concerns and provide consistent answers.

Celebrate the past and then let it go

If the outgoing headteacher is leaving for good reasons, it's great to recognise the success they brought to the school. Have a celebration that recognises the history of the school, what the headteacher has achieved and give people a chance to reflect. For example, you could create a book that all the students contribute to, which is ultimately printed and given to parents. It could even be a family focused school event with fun activities and cake!

Then start the closure process and move on. Talk about the new world (any plans for the future the new headteacher already has), the school vision and introduce the new headteacher more and more until you reach the cut-off point when they start in their new role.

Coming out the other side

Work with the new headteacher to develop a 90-day communication plan. This plan should include ensuring the new headteacher meets key people and has appropriate opportunities to listen and share views on the future. This could be through a range of activities, such as:

- Parent discussion meetings, where parents learn more about the person who will run their child's school and have an opportunity for questions.

- Teacher meetings, where teachers get to meet the new headteacher and share hopes and concerns for the future.

- Student 'meet the headteacher' sessions, where students get to share what they like about the school and what they would change.

- Media interviews with local newspapers and radio stations to introduce the headteacher to the local community.

- On the school website, where a video from the new headteacher can be posted in which they share their hopes and dreams for the school.

- On social media where daily insights from the headteacher can be posted in which they share stories as they go.

Managing change well requires a combination of all of the best-practice guidelines that we have shared so far. There are a few more specific communication areas that we discuss in the next two chapters. The first one regards communicating well when crisis hits.

Top three take-aways:

1 Understand how people react to change.

2 You can short cut how quickly people go through the change curve through planned communication.

3 Work with your leadership team to build clear and consistent messages and be visible and active in communicating as one team.

When crisis hits

Crises can come in many shapes and sizes. Aside from the obvious disaster-type scenarios of a fire or flood, there are other damaging disasters that an insurance policy will not put right, such as those that will impact the reputation of your school.

Managing communication during a crisis is about doing two things. Firstly, it's about ensuring that teachers and students are kept safe by having the right information given to them at the right time in the right way. This is what will traditionally be included in your crisis management process. Secondly, it is about managing the reputation of your school for the long term. This is often not included in a crisis management process. Managing your reputation for the long term is the focus of this chapter.

Plan in advance

You can and should plan for the unexpected. You have regular fire drills to test the fire alarms and evacuation procedures. You should also have a crisis plan in place that has been tested and is ready to go should you need to communicate quickly with your teaching staff, parents, governors, the media or anyone else.

This crisis plan is a mini-communication plan much like the larger one that you will have developed for your school. The key difference here is that time is of the essence and activities are condensed. If the press are on your doorstep or parents are gathering outside your office you won't have time to dot i's and cross t's.

Once you have your crisis communication plan, you should ensure that all staff members read and understand it. You should review and test it (in practical exercises) at regular intervals and ensure that any updates are clearly communicated to everyone involved. Finally, a copy of your crisis communication plan should be readily available in a safe place, such as the staff room, as well as other appropriate areas both in and outside the school.

Managing your reputation through a crisis

As part of your crisis management plan you will know who is responsible for various aspects of the plan. One of these aspects will be communication. The responsible person should have immediate access to all pre-drafted messages, mailing lists and communication tools that will be used.

The nature of the crisis will determine who needs to be informed and when. There is no right or wrong answer to this, as it will be specific to you and your school. The important aspect is to ensure that you respond quickly, honestly and in a way that protects the reputation of your school.

Here are seven steps you should go through with members of your team to prepare your crisis communication plan for long-term protection of your reputation:

1 Identify the different types of crisis that could happen

2 Identify their potential impact on your reputation

3 Identify which people are most likely to care about the crisis

4 Identify how you communicate with those people

5 Agree who is responsible for communication

6 Draft your messages

7 Establish crisis management communication principles

Identify the different types of crisis that could happen

These will be the more obvious ones, such as fire and flood, to the less obvious but still damaging to your reputation, such as child-protection issues, a student is attacked or attacks another person at school or an extremely poor and unexpected school inspection outcome.

Identify their potential impact on your reputation

One way to identify the impact of a crisis is using a simple grid, with 'Impact on reputation' on one side and 'Likelihood' on the other. The events that are most likely and will have the biggest impact on your reputation are the ones that you prioritise in your planning.

Identify which people are most likely to care about the crisis

There are some events that will potentially trigger more media coverage than others. For example, a student attack is likely to trigger national press coverage and interest compared to a poor Ofsted report. There are some events that parents will be more concerned about regarding their child's safety, and some, where they will voice their concerns more openly than others. For each type of crisis that you have identified, you should determine who you would communicate with in order to manage your reputation.

Identify how you communicate with those people

This may not be the same as your day-to-day communications with each audience. For example, your website may not be the quickest way to reach parents during the daytime, especially if they have heard about your crisis on the news first.

Agree who is responsible for communication

Again, this may not be the same as for day-to-day communications. This needs to be aligned with your overall crisis management plan, as there is usually a single person responsible for coordinating communications to all audiences.

Draft your messages

You won't be able to completely write each message ahead of time, but you can likely put 80 per cent of the content in there to save you time, leaving space as needed. Each audience's requirements will be different, but in principle you need messages that cover each of the following stages:

1 Notification of the crisis

2 Updates stating how it is being managed

3 Confirmation of closure

4 Next steps to avoid or reduce future risk

   Examples of such key messages are provided in Appendix 13.1.

Establish crisis management communication principles

During a crisis, more than at any other time, what people say and to whom could convey messages that may prove damaging to your school's reputation. To avoid such issues or staff speaking to the wrong people, it is advisable to have in place simple communication principles that everyone must agree and adhere to.

   Here are some factors to consider when developing your principles:

1 Who will be allowed to speak with the press on behalf of the school?

2 Who will deputise for this person in their absence?

3 Certain details, such as names of people involved, should not be divulged.

4 Statements given should be based on facts.

5 Speculation and personal opinions should be avoided.

6 Who will ensure unwanted visitors, such as press officers, are kept off site?

7 Do not share details via personal social media accounts.

A crisis communication plan template and crisis management communication principles are provided in Appendices 13.2 and 13.3, respectively.

After the crisis

Depending on what happened, your school may never be the same again. If you had an issue regarding child protection or a scathing Ofsted report, for example, it will take time and effort to rebuild trust in your school. It is important to be open and honest while sticking to your principles about stating facts not conjecture. You may need to review your annual communication plan as a result and undertake specific interventions to rebuild or maintain trust such as having open days for parents or communicating more regularly on the specific topic of your crisis. In the next chapter, we focus on another crucial area for your school – communicating inclusively.

Top three take-aways:

1 Plan now how you will communicate in a crisis, before it is too late.

2 After ensuring that everyone is safe, managing your reputation is critical.

3 Have communication principles in place and agreed on to avoid unnecessary issues.

14 Communicating inclusively

Do you communicate inclusively? Does your school? We have already spoken about communicating in ways that recognise different communication preferences, such as visual, auditory and kinaesthetic communication, and different ways of processing information, such as introvert versus extrovert processing. But recognising communication differences with regard to people of various backgrounds, beliefs, origins, disabilities, language spoken, or even sexual preferences is important, too. *Inclusive communication* means sharing information in a way that everybody can understand, regardless of these differences. This chapter discusses how to adopt a more inclusive approach to your communication.

People

The Internet and modern technology of today make it is possible to work with anyone anywhere in the world. In schools, the model is still fairly reliant on students being physically present in a classroom, so the 'anywhere in the world' scenario isn't a reality just yet, although some schools do operate virtually already. However, the impact of modern society on the students of today is that they come from a wider walk of life.

Language

Language is often the first barrier when considering inclusive communication. Even for those who speak the same language, there are often communication issues that stem from the misunderstanding of terms and phrases. There are online tools and apps, such as Culture Wizard's cross-cultural training, to help you to understand how to communicate more inclusively with other cultures.

Culture

An interesting point when thinking about culture is that each of us is already conditioned by the values and norms of our own culture that we are probably not aware of. This affects how we perceive things, and therefore how we communicate, having implications both inside and outside the classroom. For example, in some cultures, it is normal for there to be long silences within a conversation. In other cultures, it is acceptable to interrupt. If you put both of these together, without context, you will have a frustrating outcome!

Culture is not the only element to consider when aiming for inclusive communication, though. As mentioned at the start of this chapter, other factors, such as religion and disability, affect how we communicate.

Seven tips to help you communicate inclusively

Here are seven tips to help you communicate inclusively with your colleagues, parents and students:

1 Be flexible and open

2 Speak slowly and use a normal tone of voice

3 Be sensitive to nonverbal cues

4 Write down and share written work in advance

5 Be supportive

6 Make it easy for them to speak

7 Listen actively – don't interrupt

Be flexible and open

Aim to communicate on their terms, not yours. If someone has an impairment that prohibits him or her from using a computer or necessitates longer read-times or a break time, be flexible enough to give them the time and space to do so. Accommodate people's needs to avoid undue duress.

Speak slowly and use a normal tone of voice

When speaking with non-native speakers, be sure to speak slowly (although not in a condescending way). Speak clearly in your normal tone of voice and avoid using jargon or terms that are colloquial.

Be sensitive to nonverbal cues

Some cultures value silence or do not encourage lingering eye contact. In others, physical touch is frowned upon. These are important nonverbal aspects of one's communication style to be aware of.

Write down and share written work in advance

An easy way to ensure that your audience is more likely to understand your message is to write it down and send it to them in advance. This gives them time to understand it and formulate a response. There are even software tools available that will automatically translate text into another language, such as Schoop.

Be supportive

For some people, communicating directly with a teacher or headteacher is likely to be uncomfortable – particularly in cultures where rank is important. Aim to be understanding and put them at ease – smile, use supportive words and avoid anything that is too directive, if possible.

Make it easy for them to speak

Be clear that you want their views – no matter how they share them. Provide as many options as possible to gather feedback in the easiest way possible. Consider aspects such as access to the Internet, ability to travel and native language. These are all areas that can make it as easy for them to communicate with you as possible.

Listen actively – don't interrupt

Listening actively is more than just listening. It is about being fully present in mind and body. If you are thinking about the next lesson while a parent is struggling to explain their concerns for their child, it is likely you won't be able to help them properly. Smile, nod, lean in and use appropriate hand gestures to let them know you are listening and understand.

We hope this chapter has helped in achieving a better understanding of how to communicate more inclusively within your school. In the next chapter, we address how you can put what you have learned in all the preceding chapters into action.

Top three take-aways:

1 Now more than ever it is important to ensure the way you communicate is understood and accessible to everyone.

2 Don't assume people see and understand from the same point of view as you have.

3 Make an effort to communicate inclusively when dealing with audiences that are different to you in some way.

15 Put it into action

It is time to turn from theory to practice. In this chapter, we guide you through how to develop your communication action plan. It's important to have a communication action plan for a number of reasons, including the following:

- You'll have an agreed-on and sustainable plan to support improved communication in your school, rather than one-off hits of ad hoc activity that have limited impact. You can agree on this document with your leadership team and share relevant parts with other members of staff so they can proactively support key areas of the plan.

- You can be planned in your approach to activities so you can maximise opportunities around the school calendar and key events rather than trying to follow up things that are happening at the last minute. This will also save you time in the long run.

- You will drive improved effectiveness of leadership and management within your school. A key element of school inspections is to ensure that schools have a motivated, respected and effective teaching staff to deliver a high quality education for all pupils.

- You can demonstrate actions you have taken and are currently taking to Ofsted or ISI to improve leadership communication skills, such as creating and communicating a compelling vision for schools. You'll have improved student outcomes and better results because teachers will be more motivated, and this has a direct impact on students' performance. You will also drive better results through a stronger parent–school partnership.

- You can maximise your traditional marketing budget by strengthening what you do through teacher and parent advocacy. You should be able to reduce the marketing budget through taking different approaches to building your reputation. This will be more believable communication rather than paid-for advertising. You will be able to measure the return on investment of anything you spend, whether that is financially or time related, through having strong communications objectives that you track over time.

■ You'll be able to use more up-to-date communication techniques in tune with our changing world, creating new expectations and opportunities. You will better attract, motivate and retain great teachers through other methods other than pure pay. People will hear about what it is like to work at your school through the grapevine. A planned approach to inspirational leadership and great communication will encourage more teachers to come and work with you.

What should your communication plan look like?

We've provided a template for you to use (see Appendix 15.1) and steps to think through as you complete it.

1 **What do you want to achieve with your communication efforts?**
At this point, you should have carried out a fair amount of listening to your stakeholders and understand where you are now and where you want to be. Take all this great input and develop clear communication goals that are as measurable as possible. For example:

■ 80 per cent of teachers will be rated a 3 or more (1–5 rating) by parents when asked about their communication skills.

■ 90 per cent of teachers will be able to explain our vision when asked.

■ We'll reduce our top talent teacher turnover by x per cent.

■ 80 per cent of parents would recommend our school to others (3 or more on a 1–5 rating).

■ 80 per cent of parents believe we listen to their ideas and views.

2 **What do you want your school to stand for?**
We've talked a lot about vision. This is where you commit it to writing. Why should people work at your school and why should people send their children to you? What makes you unique, and can you deliver on this promise, i.e. the proof points? Keep this simple and succinct, but ensure it connects with people. It's not enough to be the best. That isn't going to get people out of bed in the morning and wanting to come to work. They want to make a difference. That's why they went into teaching in the first place. Capture that passion in your vision and you'll have a powerful North Star to guide everything you do, and something everyone can believe in.

3 **Who are you targeting with your communication approach?**
You need to be clear who your main target audiences are and who the other audiences are that you need to communicate with. For example:

- Primary target audiences: existing parents; teachers; students; other employees at the school; potential parents; and Board of Governors

- Secondary target audiences: local community; other school leaders; local media; relevant social media outlets (e.g. Mumsnet) and local businesses

Think about where each audience is right now and how important they are to your success to prioritise where you put your efforts. The more you can understand what they currently know, feel and do, the easier it is to take action and move them to where you want them to be. See Chapter 6 about understanding your audiences, and use a two-by-two graph to plot where they are and where you want them to be. You can also refer to Appendix 6.1.

Work out for each audience what you want them to do and why. In other words, define the concrete actions you want them to take. What would be the call to action for each? For example, you may encourage parents to talk about a specific topic within your school or with friends and family, or encourage teachers to talk positively in social media, guided by your social media guidelines. Think about how you'll measure whether action has been taken.

4 How will you reach the audiences?

So you know what you want to achieve, who you need to target and now you need to work out how you will target them.

Here are a few ideas for your target audiences:

Teachers:

- Develop a **'speak out' teacher group** as representatives for the broader teachers to bring ideas and opinions to support the improvement of the school.

- Have **regular teacher meetings** to discuss changes and topics – focus on inspiring and listening at these meetings.

- Use an **internal online platform** – share resources, webinars and external articles to build communication skills. Develop a forum where you can listen to ongoing ideas and feedback from teachers.

New parents:

- Develop a **parent–school partnership agreement** that is completed in discussion with each new parent that you can refer to on an ongoing basis. It should explain what is required of parents, students and the school, and manage their expectations for school communication, i.e. when to contact teachers and how to find information or share views. (See Appendix 15.2).

Existing parents:

- Create an **open door policy** at certain times of the day for parents to come in and speak to you. You may feel you already encourage this, but having to make an appointment to come see you doesn't always create that open environment.

- Develop a **video each month**, hosted on your online platform, including you speaking to students and teachers and parents talking about what is going on at the school. This will reinforce your reputation, but in a way where your internal advocates tell the story rather than just you. You could reuse elements of these to share with potential parents.

- As part of your **online platform**, **create a parent community** to provide tailored and relevant information about their children. Create opportunities to ask questions and share concerns. Address concerns openly to all parents recognising issues and saying what you are doing about them.

- Create **a traffic light system** of day-to-day communication, and have one person in the school to coordinate this. Red for 'you must read it now', amber for 'important but not urgent' and green for 'nice to know'. This can be carried across all your communication channels. You would want to send your red communication in a way that is pushed at people and goes to mobile devices, such as text or via app notifications. But remember to ask people if they received the communication as a check to understand what information is getting through.

In addition, think about yourself and your teaching employees as a channel to communicate. How effective are you/they at the moment, and what skills do you need to develop?

5 What are you going to say?

You know what people think about you and your school. You know your strengths and weaknesses and you know where you want to get to. But what do you want to say to people to help them understand your vision and direction? What do you want to say to teachers to inspire and motivate them? How can you demonstrate that the school is moving along and making progress on its path?

Here are some ideas to help you:

- **Creating stories to bring your vision to life:** Reflect on who your audiences are and where you need them to be. Although you have defined your vision, the way you bring this to life for potential parents or for a teacher may be slightly different. Think about some examples of where you know you are already delivering on this vision. Develop stories you could tell that demonstrate these examples in ways that will resonate with different people.

- **Focused messages with a call to action:** What might you need for parents, teachers, and other staff to do at different points in the year to support the students' education and to build the reputation of the school?

- **Reinforcing success stories and thought leadership:** Share leading-edge thinking with education networks (social media), share student success stories in the local media (from a sporting event or a previous student who has achieved great success) by building up relationships with your local journalists, work with local businesses to build partnerships and 'piggyback' off their campaigns where you have worked together. Support national campaigns like those to support literacy worldwide and build a sense of social responsibility and goodwill.

- **Campaigns:** You may want to consider building specific campaigns around fundraising for building projects or new equipment. This requires specific marketing techniques, but can again be driven through teacher, student and parent advocacy using social media and events.

You can put together a calendar or messages that you want to share via various communication channels, including through social media, to ensure you keep your messaging regular, planned and focused on your vision and outcomes.

6 Bringing it all together

To bring it all together, develop a week-by-week plan with activities, dates, outcomes for each activity and who will make them happen. See Appendix 15.1 for an activity schedule template.

7 Measuring success

This is one of the most important parts of the action plan. Keep measuring back against what you want to achieve and discuss the results with your leadership team. Include statistics from your online tools (number of people who use it, the most visited areas, the amount of feedback/ideas received) and from social media (number of positive school mentions compared to negative and neutral) and media coverage (number of articles and circulation of newspaper and tone of article), as well as feedback from parents and teachers and how you responded to this.

Gather information about why people send their children to your school and why they take them away. Ask parents via a poll or email survey on a regular basis (as part of other communication) – on a scale of 1–10 (10 being the highest rating), how likely they are to recommend your school. This question is crucial and is used by most organisations to measure advocacy, often referred to as a 'net promoter score'.

Review how you are doing by asking this simple question at least every 3 months. Ideally, you need an ongoing process to measure success in order to spot issues and address these quickly, or similarly, to celebrate successes rather than wait for the next quarterly measurement survey. Talk about where you are against your goals with your leadership team.

If things worked well then what made it a success? Can you do more of this? If it didn't work well then what can you learn for the future? Recognise progress and keep everyone motivated to play their part and stay on track. We look in more detail at measuring whether you are succeeding in the next chapter.

Top three take-aways:

1 Set communication objectives for your school.

2 Agree on your key messages (story/vision based).

3 Measure and review your progress regularly.

Case study: Finding new ways to partner with parents

In the example of Caledonia Primary in Glasgow, award-winning headteacher Sheona Allen is motivated by a purpose to make a difference in the lives of others. She leads a project called "Families in Partnership" that targets parents and their children who are in need of support. It culminates in a residential at an outdoor centre in the North of Scotland. Sheona and her school team participate voluntarily. The parents value the adventure that helps them to support their own child while building improved stronger relationships with the school and community.

16 Are you succeeding?

If you are clear about where you are trying to get to, then it is important to regularly check that you are still on the right track towards your destination. Measuring progress gives you and your team encouragement that you are on the right path, even if it feels difficult and frustrating at times. It also gives you some evidence of success that you can share if challenged about what you are doing. In the previous chapter when we talked about putting it into practice we started to look at how to measure success. In this chapter we provide a comprehensive list of ways in which to measure communication effectiveness against your school's vision.

How to measure progress

Some people take the approach of a moment in time 'snapshot' survey, such as a big annual survey. This is time consuming and may result in lots of actions that you can't realistically deliver. Instead, measure continually using a variety of methods and make small changes along the way.

You can measure formally and informally, and focus on both quantitative and qualitative elements. The best approach is to mix these using some of the following methods:

Survey – paper or electronic

This is a formal quantitative or qualitative approach that can be targeted to specific groups, e.g. parents of specific children. It is repeatable which means that you can compare previous surveys and set targets to achieve for future surveys. It is best practice to share a summary of the results with those who were invited to participate. You should ensure that whether you choose to do this using paper on online, your audience is able to respond.

Focus group

This is a formal qualitative approach that you can carry out with an audience of your choice. Focus groups provide a huge amount of insight and with the help of a skilled facilitator, allow you to dig deep below the surface to uncover issues. They require preparation and follow up.

Online poll

These are an easy method of measuring success that will provide a snapshot of a specific topic through your website. You need to remember though; the sample will not be representative, as it's self-selecting rather than random. It is a good idea to offer a comments section with an online poll to enable people to expand on their response, which can in turn help you better understand their position.

Parent champions

You could ask specific parents who you know are influential within their parent group and who would be willing to speak out. These may be either formally in such a role or not. This type of feedback would have to be considered as informal and is indicative requiring formal follow up. It can be a useful way to identify issues early before they escalate.

Open Q&A session

You could use a parent evening or other parent gathering to allow them to ask questions of you and your school. This is a great way to identify where there are gaps in their understanding or a lack of clarity with specific issues. This could also take place online.

Social media

Monitor social media channels to see what is being said about your school. You could do this yourself or employ a specialist agency to do it for you.

Results and applications

Ultimately, the true measure of success is improved exam results and being oversubscribed. Success in these areas is often a good benchmark that you are communicating effectively.

However you choose to measure how you are doing, you need to take actions on the results that you receive. Measurement should be a habit that is built into your approach. In the next chapter, we talk more about creating good habits to support your communication.

Top three take-aways:

1 Measure progress often as this is easier and more useful.

2 Use a variety of quantitative and qualitative techniques.

3 Use feedback to make continual improvements to your communication.

 # Create good habits

Once you have taken the steps outlined in previous chapters of this book, it is important to make those a good habit and not to allow your school to fall back into previous bad habits of poor communication. In this chapter, we describe how to create the habit of good communication within your school, by engaging with your local community, parents, teachers, students and the local media. We also cover the important element of reviewing and recognising progress.

Review regularly

Have regular formal review points where you check that you are on track to achieve the communication objectives that you set out to achieve. These should take place with a set of agreed people who will give an honest appraisal and not just tick boxes. The purpose of such a review is to help you to make changes if needed or to confirm that you are on the right track. You should build into this review process some of the measures of success discussed in Chapter 16.

Identify what worked well and what you would do differently in the future. Work out the specific actions you'll take (and who will make them happen) to put these lessons learned into practice.

Be open about how you are doing

Once you have held your communication review, share the outcomes. Firstly, share them with your teaching staff and those who work in your school. This should be your number one priority. Then share with the other people to whom you are accountable.

Recognise how far you've come

Celebrate success and share learning in equal measure. It's sometimes easy to focus on how much more you need to do, but reflect back and ensure everyone understands how far you have come from your starting point. Continue to inspire and motivate people, even if it is clear there is still much to achieve.

Recognise those people who have helped you to get there, and you'll create even more energy amongst individuals who want to play their part in moving you forward.

Engage with your local community

Working with the local community is crucial to the success of any school but also to ensuring positive student outcomes. Ensure you have activities in your communication plan that builds community advocates. This following section suggests ways to do just that.

School community days

Have school community days where groups from the local community are invited to see school events, such as senior citizen groups who could come and see a special performance of your school nativity.

Sponsorship

If funds allow, then sponsor the occasional local event so your school name is increasingly recognised but also associated with a positive community event. Pick your events carefully to ensure you build your reputation by being associated with the right things.

Students in the community

A number of schools have links out to the community to mutually benefit students and local groups or individuals. These include working with the disabled, animals or the elderly. There are also lots of opportunities for students to do work experience in local businesses, charities or help with local projects to clean up community areas or even contribute to projects to build local facilities. You could reach out to parents to see if they have skills that they could offer to also work on these projects with the children.

This will create a real sense of what your school is about, while building great skills for your students. You will potentially also benefit from some good local media coverage and you can promote this 'good citizen' work on your website or in social media.

Importantly, these initiatives build relationships with the local community. So if you ever need to put in planning permission for a new building or something goes wrong then you will find people are more supportive in helping you in the future.

Engage parents in their children's education

Students are more successful if schools engage with and work in partnership with parents. Here are some ideas to help you to reach out to parents and continue that partnership.

Encourage drop-in sessions

Hold regular drop-in sessions where parents can learn more about how to inspire their children to learn. These focus on helping children (and parents) to enjoy learning, including practical activities to bring subjects like Maths and English to life.

You can also run these to support parents with their own personal skills, such as English as a foreign language. These sessions will create a positive experience of the school for parents and build a sense of school community and even advocacy, again supporting better student outcomes.

'Remember me' wipe boards

Outside each classroom have a wipe board where teachers can quickly write up items that are needed that day or week. Students can be encouraged to look at these themselves but parents can also double-check them. If you have the technology, then you could also have a virtual wipe board on your school website or app.

New parent 'buddy' scheme

When you're the parent of a new child, it's great to know you have someone to turn to who understands how the school works. The 'buddy' scheme means that you can match up willing volunteers from higher up the school with new parents to guide them through the first few weeks more smoothly. Also ask the existing parents to share back anything they hear from the new parents so you can learn and improve.

New parent starter pack

All new parents should have a pack of clear and simple information at least signposting where to find what they need on the website, if not printed. They should also sit with a teacher and their child and discuss the parent, student and school partnership agreement. This can manage expectations of what is required from all parties and ensure everyone plays their part, avoiding issues further down the line.

Parent forums

Parent forums can be monthly meetings around specific topics of interest to both parents and the school. You can ask parents for questions before the session and then answer some of those at the forum meeting. This can then form a further discussion to dispel rumours and ensure information is clear and understood.

Parent teach-ins

Teachers can share some of the topics that are the basis for school learning. These should be as practical as possible. They could include how we learn in different ways, how to manage difficult behaviour, managing stress during exam time, Internet safety, preparing for the working world or supporting children through growing up, e.g. puberty, adolescence.

Keep engaging your teachers

In order to attract, engage, and retain teachers, they need to feel valued, be supported, be able to have their say and be continually developed. Here are some suggestions to keep the momentum going.

Teacher 'work it out' sessions

Teachers will know the issues in your school. They are often best placed to find answers to these issues. Encourage and empower them to come up with ideas, through 'work it out' sessions, to address these, giving them access to present and share their solutions with the leadership team. Show them that you value their expertise and put their ideas into practice wherever possible.

Teacher 'buddy' scheme

When a teacher starts at the school, assign him or her to a 'buddy' teacher to help get acquainted with the school and its ins and outs. Make being a teacher mentor something to be proud of. If you are part of a multi-academy trust or similar, then identify buddy teachers across different schools so that you can learn from one another and both teachers, and schools, can benefit.

Teacher team building and skills development

In addition to the regular teacher development, incorporate team building exercises that help teachers to understand one another's working preferences. Consider those where you gain insights into working and communication styles so people can understand the strengths across the team and appreciate one another's differences. Look to close any gaps where you have them, through development or future recruitment.

Teacher well-being programme

Ideally, you would have a school well-being programme (across all staff and students), but you should also have a focus on teacher well-being. Teachers can role-model great habits that will be seen by the students, who will see them setting the standard. Consider sharing practical well-being tips and talks from local specialists. You may even have some parents (or teachers) who are health, nutrition or fitness experts, who would be happy to offer their time.

Teacher recognition

We've talked about saying thank you, but something a little more formal might be appreciated. You could have term-based awards, such as best teacher idea, and some less formal recognition such as hand-written thank you notes. However, we recommend that you recognise people in ways they themselves are comfortable with and that have meaning to them rather than handing out lots of public praise (which can be embarrassing for some).

Engage your students

Students should have a voice in the running of your school. Here are some suggestions for how you can involve them and keep your good communication habits going.

Student council

Students and staff elect members to the student council. Those students become a voice on behalf of other students on some decisions in the school. This gives a strong message that you value the opinions of students, if you handle this well, with clear guidelines to manage expectations.

Student forums

You can have online or verbal forums where students come together around specific topics to share their views. Again, you need 'etiquette' guidelines and to manage expectations. Student forums create a great opportunity to listen and gather ideas. You can also have online quick polls that give students options to choose from to give you a 'temperature check' on any topic.

Student journalists

Encourage students to be journalists to contribute to and produce a student newspaper, create school TV programmes and contribute to what is on your website. Set them projects like 'What's great about our school?'. This could create some useful outputs and will also give students good skills for the future.

Keep going by engaging with the local media

Don't wait until you have a success story or issue to handle before contacting the local media. Try any of these suggestions below to keep your momentum going.

Journalist open day

Build relationships by proactively showing journalists around your school. Introduce them to students to hear what it is like at the school and let them better understand your direction and dreams for how the school can flourish. Understand more about what types of stories they may be interested in. Find out if you can work on a longer term series of articles or feature story.

Put a spotlight on your experts

If you are keen to raise your profile in the education media, you could provide a list of teacher 'experts' who can talk about particular subjects. They will probably need some media training to support them in handling the journalists' questions. This could position your school as a thought leader.

Having moved through the previous chapters and steps, it is time to move on to the final chapter: You're ready to go.

Top three take-aways:

1 Tell all of your stakeholders about your new communication approach.

2 Be open and honest about your successes and challenges.

3 Be creative and look for the many opportunities to engage with your key stakeholders.

Case study: Working with local businesses for mutual benefit

In the example of Yarrells School in Dorset, the school worked with local businesses, including an architect, to build a new classroom block "Greenwood". The headmaster, Andrew Roberts-Wray, devotes time to networking with entrepreneurs to create this symbiotic relationship with local businesses. He knows that this will help the school, including through students being able to develop an understanding of the real world. It also helps local businesses because the students are their future employees.

18 You're ready to go

Now you have the tools you need to put everything you've learned into action. It is not just for today or for the next month, but for the long term. Here is a quick reminder of the key steps to communication success for your school already covered in this book:

1 **Listen** to what people currently think about your school – the good, bad and ugly.

2 **Agree** with your team what your school stands for (**your vision**) and ensure you can all believe in this and live it every day.

3 **Identify communication actions** to close the gap between your vision and what people experience on a daily basis, such as teachers, governors, parents, students and the local community. Develop a clear communication plan with agreed delivery dates and owners.

4 **Know the main audiences** who you should involve and inform, who will influence the success of your school.

5 **Put systems and processes in place** to communicate well with these audiences, understanding their needs while supporting the goals for your school.

6 **Listen** to what your audiences say on an ongoing basis.

7 Tell people that you've listened and you are taking/have taken action to build trust and **encourage future feedback**.

8 **Develop communication skills** across your school, including those of teachers, students, your own personal skills and those of your leadership team.

9 **Monitor feedback and results** and take action to improve your communication for the future.

There is clearly a lot to do if you want to really role model great communication, in a sustainable way. It takes time and effort to create the right framework and policies, and you will need a level of dedicated resource to ensure communication is managed effectively.

You are not alone

You may want to consider employing external expertise to at least put the framework in place. An external perspective can sometimes help you to spot issues that may not be so obvious when you are 'in the thick of things'. Your internal team are also more likely to accept new ways of working when they are introduced by external specialists, rather than someone internal to your school.

Whichever route you choose, we wish you the very best of luck! We hope that this book has helped you to create and sustain communication success within your school. We have written this book with the support of teachers for teachers. Successful communication in school makes a difference to them, to you, to the future of education and most of all to our children – both those of today and in the future.

Top three take-aways:

1 Communication is an opportunity to differentiate your school – take it!

2 Listen before you start.

3 Consider using external experts to complement the knowledge, skills and resources available in your school.

Bibliography

Actual Minds, Possible Worlds, Jerome S. Bruner (1986).

Audio-Visual Methods in Teaching, Edgar Dale (1969).

The Business Case for Employees Health and Wellbeing: A report prepared for investors in people UK, Stephen Bevan (2010).

Concept of Employee Engagement: An analysis based on the Workplace Employment Relations Study, MacLeod and Clarke (2014).

The Culture Cycle: How to shape the unseen force that transforms performance, James Heskett (2011).

Digital Yearbook, Simon Kemp, We Are Social (2016).

Emotional Intelligence, Daniel Goleman (1995).

The Evidence: Wellbeing and engagement, Engage for Success (2014).

Fit2Communicate Limited, Research with parents of school age children (2014–15).

The Impact of Employee Engagement on Performance, Harvard Business Review Analytic Services (2013).

The Impact of Parental Involvement, Parental Support and Family Education on Pupil Achievements and Adjustment: A literature review, C. Desforges with A. Abouchaar, DfES Research Report 433 (2003).

Improving Employee Performance in the Economic Downturn, Corporate Leadership Council/Corporate Executive Board (2008).

Ketchum Leadership Communication Monitor (2014).

National Standards of Excellence for Headteachers, Department for Education (2015).

Review of Best Practice in Parental Engagement, Janet Goodall and John Vorhaus with Jon Carpentieri, Greg Brooks, Rodie Akerman and Alma Harris, Research Report Dfe-RR156 (2010).

Six Components of a Great Culture, John Coleman, Harvard Business Review (2013).

Stimulus Modality and Verbal Learning Performance in Normal Aging. Brain and Language, Constantinidou and Baker (2002).

Trends in Global Employee Engagement, Aon Hewitt (2012).

Visual Learners Convert Words to Pictures in the Brain and Vice Versa, Says Psychology Study, University of Pennsylvania (2009).

Appendix 2.1

Fit2Communicate survey results

Q1: Please rate how well your child's school keeps you informed about the important things you need to know.

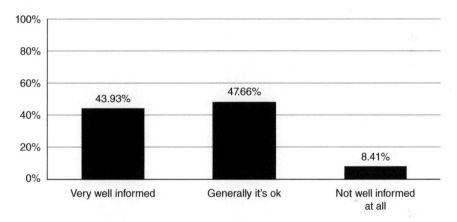

Q2: What areas could your child's school improve to keep you better informed? (You can choose more than one answer.)

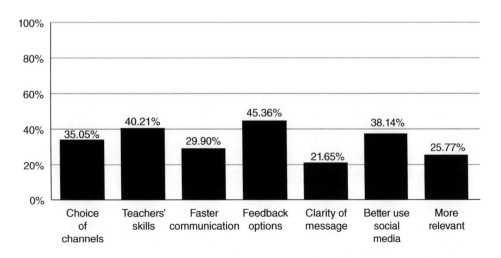

Q3: When considering which school your child should go to, how important is it that the school communicates well with parents?

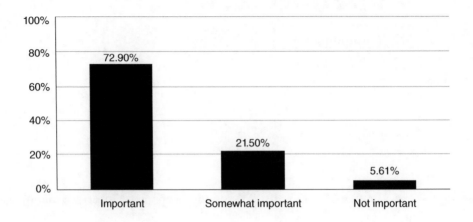

Appendix 4.1

SWOT analysis for schools template

A SWOT analysis is an extremely useful and quick method for getting a snapshot of your school's current situation. SWOT is an acronym for Strengths, Weaknesses, Opportunities, Threats. Completing a SWOT analysis can be done individually or with the input of the school leadership team in a brainstorming approach. It can provide a good opportunity for team building and valuable discussion.

Traditionally, Strengths and Weaknesses are regarded as internal factors, whereas Opportunities and Threats are regarded as external factors. However, when carrying out the SWOT for your school, we suggest you do not limit the analysis to only internal and external factors when considering the four elements. For example, you may be opening a new site for your school, which provides an opportunity for many things but is internal to your school.

In the template provided, we have included some suggestions for areas you can consider as part of your analysis. This is not intended to be a definitive list and you should challenge yourself and your team to create a complete SWOT analysis that is relevant and specific for your school at a moment in time.

Make sure to state the date of the analysis, as over time the factors will change. You may also wish to compare to previous years to see if you have turned weaknesses into strengths and threats into opportunities. There is no right or wrong answer to this exercise but it does provide a focus, once agreed, of areas to work on.

Name of school_____

Date of SWOT analysis_____

Strengths	Weaknesses
• What makes your school unique? • Do you have a strong track record of results? • Are your teachers engaged? • Are your students happy? • Are parents actively involved in the school? • Are you financially stable? • Are you positioned in a favourable geographical position? • Have you won awards or external recognition? • Are your systems and processes for communication working well? • Do you have low teacher turnover? • Do you have a good inspection report?	• What is your school missing that other schools have? • Are your results in decline or stagnant? • Are students unhappy? • Are parents disengaged? • Are you struggling financially? • Are there lots of other schools around you who are 'better'? • Is communication regularly breaking down? • Is discipline good enough, consistently? • Are teachers leaving your school? • Is your inspection report negative or worse than previous?
Opportunities	**Threats**
• What changes externally could you build on? • What can you do that other schools can't? • Where can you partner with other schools, colleges or businesses to provide a better experience? • Did the inspectorate highlight areas you can build on to your advantage? • Are parents open to change? • Do you have plans to expand your school or join a multi-academy trust? • Have you recently recruited teachers who are innovative? • Can you enter awards or other ways to create recognition for your school? • Do you do something that's different or unique to other schools? • Are you regularly oversubscribed?	• Will changes being imposed by government impact your school? • Are you struggling to attract new teachers to your school? • Has the inspectorate made public any areas you must improve? • Do you regularly receive negative press coverage? • Is your school shrinking while others expand or merge? • Are you regularly undersubscribed? • Have you neglected to invest in systems, which will result in issues very soon?

Appendix 4.2

Example survey questions for parents

Demographic	
1. What year is your child in?	Insert options
Perception of school brand/vision	
2. What three words would you use to describe the school right now?	Free text
3. Why did you choose this school for your child/children?	Proximity/convenience Recommendation Ofsted report Sibling(s) attended Other
4. Has your experience of the school met your expectations?	Fully Mostly A little Not at all
5. How likely are you to recommend the school as a place to send someone's children?	Very likely Likely Unlikely Not at all
Leadership	
6. Do you see the school motto being lived by the school staff?	Always Mostly Sometimes Never
7. How confident are you in the leadership of the school?	Fully Mostly A little Not at all
8. What would make you more confident in the school's leadership?	Free text

Teacher communication capability	
9. Does the communication you receive from the school enable you to make good decisions about your child's education?	Always Mostly Sometimes Never
10. How would you rate the teachers' ability to communicate directly with you?	Very good Good Poor Very poor
11. Which areas of communication could be improved?	Free text
Information flow/channels	
12. Rank, in order of importance, how you prefer to hear important and urgent news from the school.	Personal email Text message School website Letter in school bag Face to face Social media Mobile app Other
13. Rank, in order of importance, how you prefer to hear 'nice-to-know' information from the school.	Personal email Text message School website Letter in school bag Face to face Social media Mobile app Other
14. Do you feel able to share your views, concerns and questions with the right person at the school?	Always Mostly Sometimes Never
15. How would you rate the amount of information that you receive from the school?	Too much About right Not enough
General	
16. Do you have any other comments you would like to share?	Free text

Appendix 4.3

Example survey questions for teachers and governors

Perception of school brand/vision	
1. What three words would you use to describe the school right now?	Free text
2. Can you see a clear link between your work and the school's goals?	Fully Mostly A little Not at all
3. How likely are you to recommend the school as a place to send someone's children?	Very likely Likely Unlikely Not at all
Leadership	
4. How often do you feel inspired to work at the school?	Always Most of the time Sometimes Never
5. Are you proud to be a member of the school team?	Always Most of the time Sometimes Never
6. Do you feel that your views are valued?	Always Most of the time Sometimes Never
7. How likely are you to recommend the school as a place to work?	Very likely Likely Unlikely Not at all

Staff team working and training	
8. Do you have the right information to make good decisions in your work?	Always Mostly Sometimes Never
9. Do you feel equipped to communicate well with parents?	Always Mostly Sometimes Never
10. Do you feel supported in your daily work?	Always Mostly Sometimes Never
11. What made you want to become a teacher?	Free text or N/A
12. Which elements of your job put the most pressure on you?	Free text
13. Are you thinking about leaving the school? If so why?	Yes – I am actively looking Yes – But I haven't done anything about it yet No – But I would if the right offer came along No – I am here for life
Information flow/channels	
14. Rank, in order of importance, how you prefer to hear important and urgent news from the school.	Personal email Text message School website Face to face Social media Other
15. Rank, in order of importance, how you prefer to hear 'nice-to-know' information from the school.	Personal email Text message School website Face to face Social media Other
16. Are there opportunities to share ideas with your colleagues to improve the school?	Always Mostly Sometimes Never
General	
17. Do you have any other comments you would like to share?	Free text

Appendix 6.1

Understanding how far you need to move your audiences' mindset

Keeping in mind who your audiences are, you need to think about each one in terms of where they are now and where you want them to be after you have communicated your message. This template aims to support you in this thinking.

We've broken this into what you want them to think, feel and do so you can really put yourself in their shoes and understand what success would tangibly look like.

Audiences	Where are they now?			Where do we want them to be?		
	Think	*Feel*	*Do*	*Think*	*Feel*	*Do*
[Audience 1]						
[Audience 2]						
[Audience 3]						
[Audience 4]						
[Audience 5]						

Appendix 7.1

Example school media policy

Overview

Social media represents a fantastic opportunity to share positive stories and experiences about our school. It does, however, require some user guidelines to protect both the school and those using social media.

In summary, this policy is intended to:

- confirm expectations of school staff and contractors when posting on social media,

- protect the reputation of the school and those using social media, and

- provide boundaries between personal and professional lives.

Introduction

It is crucial that pupils, parents and the public at large have confidence in the school's decisions and services. The principles set out in this policy are designed to ensure that school staff and contractors use social media responsibly so that confidentiality of pupils and other staff and the reputation of the school are safeguarded.

Scope

This policy applies to all school staff and contractors, and covers personal use of social media as well as the use of social media for official school purposes, including sites hosted and maintained on behalf of the school.

Legal framework

All individuals working on behalf of the school are bound by a legal duty of confidence and other laws to protect the confidential information they have access to during the course of their work and to refrain from any activities that could be considered as harassment or discrimination.

Principles

- Avoid activities that might bring the school into disrepute.

- Avoid conflict between your work for the school and your personal interests.

- Do not represent your personal views as those of the school.

- Do not discuss and share personal information about pupils or school staff.

- Do not use social media in any way to attack, insult, abuse or defame.

- You must be accurate, fair and transparent at all times.

- Follow the standard guidelines for having contact with students and their families.

Personal use of social media

Staff members must not identify themselves as employees of the school or service providers for the school in their personal webspace.

Using social media on behalf of the school

Official school sites must be created only according to the specified requirements of this policy. Sites created must not breach the terms and conditions of social media service providers, particularly with regard to minimum age requirements.

Breaches of the policy

Any breach of this policy may lead to disciplinary action being taken against the staff member(s) involved in line with School Disciplinary Policy and Procedure.

Appendix 9.1

Building an impactful story

What is storytelling?

As humans, we like stories. They help us to connect with others and have been told since caveman times. Stories can help us to communicate and build understanding in a way that people can visualise and feel, rather than just being told information. This captures their attention and keeps them interested.

Stories are good for sharing at events, in videos, online blogs or smaller group discussions with parents, teachers or students.

Creating your story

Work through the steps below. Your story should:

■ Have a definite start, middle and end.

■ Be clear, succinct and in natural language.

■ Appeal to your audience in the theme, characters and language. Understand your audience to know what could be relevant.

■ Be delivered with energy, volume, a good tone of voice, eye contact and expressive body language. Tell your story at a good (and slightly slower) pace so you can pause and allow people to imagine what you have just described. Allow people the time to get to the place that you are transporting them to.

Step	Step explained	Example of how a teacher might use storytelling to explain to children how to overcome adversity
Who are your characters?	• Identify **strong characters** (human or animal) so you inject some personality. • The best stories are personal and talk in the **first person**. • **Be brave** (to a point where you are comfortable) and share some of your own feelings and things you have learned. • If you are talking in the **second person** then use words like 'imagine' to get the audience thinking. • Those in the **third person** ('he said') can also work but can seem more distant.	The children laughed at James' clumsy approach as he walked up the steps and onto the dusty stage. He felt like curling up into a tiny ball. Why was it always him? Why couldn't he be one of the cool kids? But he had to keep going. He had to show them. Unknown to this carpet of children, James had a hidden talent. He'd been too scared to share it before but now it was time. As he played the guitar, the room fell silent and tiny jaws dropped all around the room.
Action or conflict?	• Either the **character does something** or something happens to the character. • All stories need some **conflict or active struggle** - whether they are emotional or physical. • Make it clear what the characters have to **gain or lose**.	James' arch enemy, John Bully, was in the crowd. He'd only ever seen James as an opportunity for some misguided 'fun' but now he saw him differently and started applauding.
Adding emotion	• You need to share the **emotions of your character**. • Also build an **emotional response** among your audience. • Emotion gives the story memorable impact.	John had made James feel small and angry. He wasn't going to feel like that again. Now he was free to feel what he wanted. His heart leapt at the thought, and he played harder and harder until the song finally ended to the sound of more applause, whooping and cheering.
Painting a picture	• **Create imagery** in people's minds by bringing in well observed details into your story.	James walked out of the huge, grey school hall and into the warm, yellow sunshine. He heard the bees and saw the bright flowers in a new way. He was back and he was going to succeed at that school.

Step	Step explained	Example of how a teacher might use storytelling to explain to children how to overcome adversity
Consider throwing in a surprise	• A really memorable story may have a **great surprise that really sticks** in people's minds.	Suddenly he heard a voice behind him. It was John Bully. He was holding out his hand towards James. James looked him deep in the eye, remembering how he'd made him feel but clearly this was John's way of saying sorry. James reached out and shook John's hand. It was over. James remembered that day for the rest of his life. And whenever anyone tried to bully him again, he saw John Bully's face in his head and knew just what to do. No bully was going to get the better of him again.

Recognising this story as an example of personal triumph over adversity, other classic story lines that you may wish to use would include:

■ The adventure or journey

■ Self-discovery

■ A hero's story

Appendix 9.2

Delivering inspirational messages

How to use this template: Run through the steps in the template. Keep the steps in mind in all of your interactions, whether it is a presentation to a room full of people or a one-to-one discussion with a parent.

Even if you are doing a formal presentation, aim to make this a conversation wherever possible, because your audience will probably only have a maximum 20-minute attention span. Find ways to interact and keep them engaged.

Who is your audience?	[Be as specific as possible about who you will be speaking to.]		
What do you know about them?	[The more you know about your audience, the more you can tailor your message to them. You need to be in tune with what people are interested in so you can appeal to this and make your message relevant.]		
Your audience outcome	**Think** [What one thing do you want your audience to think after you have delivered your message?]	**Feel** [What one thing do you want your audience to feel after you have delivered your message?]	**Do** [What one thing do you want your audience to do after you have delivered your message?]
Your outcome	[If you could achieve just one thing with this communication then what would it be?]		
What environment do you want to create?	[Consider where people may have come from and their state of mind. They may have rushed from work and feel harassed, or are overloaded with lots on their minds. Take some time to make the environment comfortable and provide things like a drink or snack to create a different starting point, or perhaps try using music to set the scene.]		
How will you appeal to different types of people?	**Different ways of listening** (auditory, visual, kinaesthetic) [Can you use visuals or ask people to go through an experience to appeal to different communication types?]	**Different preferences for energy** (Introverts/ extroverts) [Introverts may prefer to have information prior to the event.]	
How will you open?	[Find a positive and immediate way to grab attention or build rapport. Share a surprising fact, ask a question, ask for a show of hands, have some fun around a topical event.]		
Your first point	Your message [Identify your first message to achieve your outcome.]	Your evidence to support this [Can you share facts or a story to bring this to life and make it real?]	
Your second point	Your message [Identify your second message to achieve your outcome.]	Your evidence to support this [Can you share facts or a story to bring this to life and make it real?]	
Your third point	Your message [Identify your third message to achieve your outcome.]	Your evidence to support this [Can you share facts or a story to bring this to life and make it real?]	
The close	[Bring what you have said to a logical close, and succinctly remind your audience what you said. This is the time to remind them of specific actions and next steps. And of course, ask for questions to check their understanding if you haven't already.]		

Now find out how you did. Ask friendly faces for their feedback and build on learning for next time.

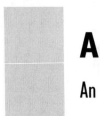

Appendix 10.1

An example to support parents in finding information

Your guide to [insert name] school information

Information you may need	Where to find it
Meet the headteacher	• Contact the headteacher by phone or email – details are on the website. • Take a look at the short video on our website.
Latest news	• See the school website, our Facebook page and Twitter feed for the latest news.
Daily updates on what's needed for learning	• See the wipe boards outside each classroom for what to bring the next day. • We encourage students to take responsibility – this information is for students and parents.
Your child's progress	• Join termly meetings with your child's teacher. • See your child's progress book, where we share progress and ideas for further learning. • Contact teachers directly via email (see website) if you have urgent questions or concerns.
School policies and rules	• These can be found on the school website. • All new parents are given a copy in their new starter pack.
Calendar of school events	• Available on the website and our school app.
Sports fixtures	• Available on the website and our school app.
Virtual learning (assisting with learning and support homework)	• Available through our website and school app.
School contact details	• Our school address, map and general phone number are on our website. • Find contact details for the headteacher and all teachers on our website.
Parent association information	• Access the section of our website for how to join, who to contact and latest news.
Parent consent forms	• These are available on the website for you to complete and return electronically.
Information for new parents	• See our website and app for new parent information and new parent liaison contacts. • You'll receive a new-parent information pack when you meet the headteacher, including policies and a parent/student/school partnership agreement to discuss and sign.
School uniform information	• Available on our website including school shop opening hours.
How to ask questions or share ideas or concerns	• Share your views on our website through quick polls, surveys and the contact page. • Contact the teacher if you have an urgent question. Email addresses are on the website. • Look out for invites to our regular parents forums where we ask for your views on various school topics.
Any last minute and urgent information	• Look out for text messages. We'll only use these for urgent information. • Less urgent but important information will be sent by email.

Appendix 12.1

Question and answer template

It's good to keep a record of the source of your questions and who answered them when you are in a crisis or change situation. You should have one source that is updated by a single person that all other people feed into. This will be a good source document for you and your leadership team.

Question	Source of question	Answer	Answered by	Date answered

Appendix 13.1

Crisis communication in schools: Key messages template

These templates are provided as a guide to enable you to draft messages in advance for your own school. They are not intended to be complete, but to save time when required. Subject to the audience, you will need to amend the message appropriately and also the method of communication.

Notification of the crisis

For the attention of [Staff / Governors / Parents / Media / Emergency Services]
On [DATE] an incident / the following incident has occurred at [SCHOOL].
INSERT DETAILS IF APPROPRIATE
Please note that at this stage we are unable to provide any more detailed information.
We will be updating our website / emergency telephone line.
A further update will follow on [DATE / TIME].
In the meantime if you have any questions please contact [INSERT].
Thank you
Headteacher

Updates on how crisis is being managed

For the attention of [Staff / Governors / Parents / Media / Emergency Services]
On [DATE] we informed you of an incident / the following incident at [SCHOOL].
INSERT DETAILS IF APPROPRIATE
Please note that we are currently working with [INSERT] to manage this incident.
We will continue to update our website / emergency telephone line.
A further update will follow on [DATE / TIME].
In the meantime if you have any questions please contact [INSERT].
Thank you
Headteacher

Confirmation of end of crisis

For the attention of [Staff / Governors / Parents / Media / Emergency Services]

On [DATE] we informed you of an incident / the following incident at [SCHOOL].

INSERT DETAILS IF APPROPRIATE

Please note that the issue has now been resolved.

The following action(s) have been taken: INSERT DETAILS

If you have any further questions please contact [INSERT].

Thank you

Headteacher

Next steps to avoid further or future risk

For the attention of [Staff / Governors / Parents / Media / Emergency Services]

On [DATE] we informed you that an incident / the following incident at [SCHOOL] had occurred and been resolved.

INSERT DETAILS IF APPROPRIATE

We have now reviewed the situation and put in place the following action to ensure this does not happen again / to reduce future risks of this nature: INSERT DETAILS

If you have any further questions please contact [INSERT].

Thank you

Headteacher

Appendix 13.2

Crisis communication plan template

Name of school: _____

Person responsible for keeping this plan up to date: _____

Last updated on: _____

Next update due on: _____

Crisis management communication team:

Overall responsible: _____

Spokesperson 1: _____

Spokesperson 2: _____

Spokesperson 3: _____

Spokesperson 4: _____

Spokesperson 5: _____

Crisis Management Communication Timeline:

Task #	Description	Responsible	Target start	Target complete	Objective
1	Holding message issued	Communication Lead	Day 0	Day 0	Inform relevant audiences of crisis.
2	Crisis-specific key messages	Communication Lead	Day 0	Day 0	Provide consistent message about crisis for school.
3	Key audiences briefed – senior team / governors / teachers / parents	Headteacher / Senior Team	Day 0	Day 0	Ensure those immediately impacted are aware.
3	Spokespeople briefed	Headteacher / Communication Lead	Day 0	Day 1	Prepare for media and other external enquiries.
4	Set up specific web page / telephone number / social media handle	Communication Lead	Day 0	Day 1	Provide dedicated way to manage queries from outside.
5	Contact media	Spokespeople	Day 0	Day 1	Engage media early to influence message.
6	Contact suppliers and other relevant parties	Communication Lead	Day 0	Day 1	Inform anyone who would be impacted indirectly.
7	Provide updates during the crisis to each audience	Headteacher / Communication Lead	Day 1		Keep everyone informed appropriately.
8	Provide closure message to each audience	Headteacher / Communication Lead			Inform everyone that crisis has closed.
9	Update the specific web page / telephone number / social media handle with the final outcome and date it will close	Communication Lead		End day	Formally close down the emergency channels and return to business as usual.
10	Provide learnings and review communication to relevant audiences	Headteacher		After end day	Confirm the crisis has ended and lessons have been learned to avoid repeat.

PLEASE NOTE:

This timeline is a guide only. It assumes a crisis that is immediate and visible hence needing to inform audiences on day 0. In the case of a less visible crisis, such as a poor inspection report, the timeline can be extended, although the steps would be the same in order to preserve the reputation of your school.

Appendix 13.3

Crisis management communication principles for schools

1 There will be a **single person who is responsible** and has oversight of all communication going in and out of the school.

2 **Parents and next of kin** to anyone involved in a crisis will be given **priority** over all other audiences.

3 Wherever possible, **fully trained experts** (e.g. emergency services personnel, family liaison officers) will speak to parents and next of kin to anyone involved in a crisis.

4 Only specific staff members who have been **formally trained** and briefed are allowed to speak to the media.

5 Staff members **must not speculate**, give personal views of the situation, or embellish facts, either in person or via social media.

6 Staff members can only **share agreed messages** and if none have been agreed then they should refer any questions to the appropriate communications representative.

7 The school will **keep relevant audiences informed** in a timely and appropriate manner.

8 If providing a **specific contact number**, email address or social media site for queries relating to the crisis, the school undertakes to monitor this and to respond in a timely and appropriate manner.

9 A **cascade briefing process** ensuring that all members of staff are appropriately informed will be followed – as a general guide it will follow the hierarchy and previously agreed principles of who should brief who.

10 All communication will be **considerate** of the situation and in particular respectful of anyone who is involved – seeking permission to communicate where appropriate.

Appendix 15.1
Your school communication plan

1 What do you want to achieve? Why are you communicating?
- What is the one outcome that you want to achieve with the delivery of this communication plan?
- How will you know when you have been successful?

2 What is your vision for your school?
- What is the agreed vision that makes you stand out from the crowd? This should run through all your messages and activities.

3 Who are you communicating with?
- Which audiences does this message need to reach (within and outside your school)? Which stakeholders do you need to influence? Where are they right now on this topic?
- What do you need them to think, feel and do for this to be successful?

4 Key messages
- What do you want people to know and understand to achieve your outcome? Should the messages be different for each audience so they have meaning, are relevant and resonate?
- Is there a broader context that your message needs to reflect, in terms of broader education trends or your wider school vision? Are there sensitivities you need to consider?
- Ensure your messages are inclusive and accessible and that you have listened enough to your audiences to understand any potential issues or opportunities to appeal to their interests and motivations.

5 How will you reach different audiences?
- Think about the audience preferences for communicating. Refer to the overview of communication channels and identify those that will help you achieve your outcomes and move them to where you need them to be.

6 Measurement of success
- How will you know if your communication was successful? What will you measure? How will you measure?
- Remember to take action on what you find out when you measure and let people know that you have listened and acted.

© Karen Dempster and Justin Robbins

7 Activity Schedule

When? Date/time	What? Your communication activity/channel	Who? *Audience* Who should receive the message	Who? *Sender* The sender of the message	The message	Who will make this happen? The activity owner who will organise and arrange sign offs	Notes/ Status
	[e.g. monthly face-to-face meeting with parents]	[e.g. Year 6 parents]	[e.g. Year 6 head of year]	[e.g. discuss common concerns raised with teachers]		[e.g. ensure this is in the evening as many parents work]

Appendix 15.2

Building your parent/student/teacher partnership agreement

A student's education has to be a partnership between the school, student and parents. It's proven that when parents are more engaged in their child's education the child achieves better results.

Often the onus is put on the school to 'deliver'. If you can agree on what parents and students should also bring to the table, then you set things off on the right foot and potentially avoid future issues and misunderstandings. After it has been signed, the school, parent and student should each have their own copy.

This contract should not be used as part of a one-off discussion. It should be discussed as part of every parent–teacher meeting, and also something that students see referred to around the school regularly in terms of repeat messaging. They obviously need consistent structure and to understand what is expected of them.

Here is an example agreement for you to tailor for your school:

[Insert name] school parent/student/school partnership agreement

Working in partnership to help each student grow to his or her fullest potential

As a representative of [insert name] school, we will:

- Show respect for each student and their family.

- Be true to our school vision, including demonstrating the right behaviours.

- Provide a safe, supportive and caring environment to support a student's learning.

- Take student concerns seriously and encourage students to have opinions to improve the school.

- Help each student to grow to his or her fullest potential.

- Enforce school and classroom rules fairly and consistently.

- Equip students to learn and make learning enjoyable.

- Work in partnership with parents to achieve the best student outcomes including:

  - Regular opportunities for discussion about every child's progress, with documented reports

  - Keeping parents informed about how they can play their part in their child's education

  - Equipping and supporting parents to reinforce the standards expected by [insert name] school

As a student, I will:

- Always try to do my best work.

- Be kind and helpful to my classmates, living our school values.

- Show respect for myself, my school and others, recognising that I represent my school even when not in school.

- Respect school rules and encourage others to do the same.

- Ask for help and share my opinions in a positive way.

- Be prepared to learn every day, with the right homework completed and right equipment.

- Believe in myself, my abilities and that I can achieve a lot more than I think.

- Look for ways to learn more, outside of school and not just homework.

- Talk with my parents each day about my school activities, what I'm enjoying and where I need help or have concerns.

As a parent/guardian, I will:

- Show respect and support for my child, the teachers and school.

- Support and reinforce the school's rules and policies with my child.

- Provide an appropriate place for my child/children to continue their learning at home.

- Attend parent–teacher discussions about my child and support agreed actions.

- Read and respond to urgent text or email messages from school and where appropriate take the necessary action.

- Refer to the [insert name] school website for information to support my child's education*.

- Talk with my child/children about what they are learning and understand what they enjoy and where they may need help so I can share this back with [insert name] school.

- Aim to take part in learning activities with my child wherever possible (e.g. reading, looking up information for projects).

--   ----------------------------

Teacher signature/date

--   ----------------------------

Student signature/date

--   ----------------------------

Parent signature/date

*See the separate information sheet that explains where you can find information you'll need to support your child's education.

Index

Page numbers in **bold** refer to tables. Page numbers in *italics* refer to figures.